BLAZING A WAGON TRAIL TO OREGON

A Weekly Chronicle of the Great Migration of 1843

Lloyd W. Coffman

Echo Books
Enterprise, Oregon

History with its flickering lamp stumbles along the trail of the past, trying to reconstruct its scenes, to revive its echoes, and kindle with pale gleams the passion of former days.
Sir Winston Churchill

ISBN 0-9635984-0-6
Library of Congress Catalog Card Number: 93-070403

Cover drawing courtesy of Scotts Bluff National Monument

Echo Books
P.O. Box 171
Enterprise, Oregon 97828

AUTHOR'S INTRODUCTION

The Oregon Trail experience has been the subject of many books during the last century and a half. I admit I have not read them all, but those I have read at least mention the Great Migration of 1843 that set everything in motion. Yet, surprisingly, no one has seen fit to make that epic adventure the subject of a book on its own. At first I assumed that it was because there was not enough primary material to make the effort worthwhile. So, as I began research for this volume I was not expecting to get far. To my delight, however, I found a considerable body of diaries, letters, and reminiscences that told a story I found fascinating. I hope to convey that fascination to you.

After several years of teaching and lecturing about the history of the Oregon Trail, I have come to the conclusion that the drama of that experience will never cease to captivate audiences of all ages. I think that is because it is such a human event. There are no famous generals, political leaders, or members of aristocracy involved, just a cast of ordinary characters that changed each year. But students find it is easy to relate to those people, they are so much like ourselves.

Throughout this book, I have purposely avoided a teaching approach beyond what I considered necessary to place events in historical perspective. Instead, it has been my plan to let the participants do the teaching as they share with us what it was like to cross the plains in 1843. I found, that by allowing the story to unfold on its own, that I did learn a lot more than I had expected. And, I gained a deep appreciation and affection for the marvelous people who had the foresight to record their thoughts and feelings for posterity. I suspect others will feel the same way.

CONTENTS

CHAPTER ONE

Catching the Fever

I

I n the fall and winter of 1842 the American economy was in an awful mess as the harshest depression of the century struck rock-bottom. According to one study, from 1839 on, "the United States . . . entered upon an era of declining prices and a succession of lean years for the farmer, so long continued that men became restless, visionary, even revolutionary." On the nation's rural frontier, which then extended as far as the western border of Missouri, an agricultural market was virtually non-existent.

Jesse Applegate, age thirty-two, lived on what had once been a prosperous farm in St. Clair County, Missouri when he became one of the restless and visionary. In the summer of 1842 he wrote his brother, "twelve months ago I labored to advance — now I struggle harder to retain my position."

Wheat was selling for twenty-five cents a bushel when it took at least fifty cents to make a profit, hogs had dropped in price from $4.20 per hundred weight in 1839 to under a dollar — if you could find a buyer. And Jesse had recently sold a steamboat load of bacon and lard for one hundred dollars when the curing salt alone cost $150. (The steamboat intended to use the bacon as fuel.)

A neighboring farmer, Daniel Waldo, age forty-three, faced the same market problems as Applegate but had accumulated enough wealth to survive a depression. Yet he, too, was restless and discontented. Not because of the economy, but because he was a sick man. And he was not alone, sickness was endemic in the land along the rivers of the Mississippi Valley.

In the mid-nineteenth century people had little idea about how disease spread. They did not realize that the mosquitoes that thrived in the river bottoms were responsible for their problems. To them, illness was inevitable; it was simply in the air. They called it ague (actually, a form of malaria, a word that meant "bad air") and the accompanying shakes and fever had become so common that many people took them for granted. Still, sufferers such as Waldo remained receptive to anything that looked like a cure.

Peter Burnett was not a farmer, nor was he ill, yet his problems paralleled those of Applegate and Waldo. He was a store-keeper in Weston, Missouri, and like all townsmen on the frontier he depended upon the farm trade. Not surprisingly, then, his business was not going well. He had sold all of his property and lived frugally but could scarcely meet the interest on his debt. To add to his woes, his wife was in delicate health and the cold weather was slowly killing her. It had been all he could do to keep her alive through the previous winter. Since she and Peter had six children, he worried about how he could care for them should she die. At age thirty-five, his future looked bleak. He, too, looked for a way out.

James Nesmith had a different reason for restlessness. Unlike Applegate, Waldo or Burnett, he had no property, health, or family problems to worry about. At age twenty-two he simply desired adventure. As he expressed it, "I was a poor, homeless youth, destitute alike of friends, money and education. Actuated by a restless spirit of adventure, one place was to me the same as another."

Four men, four reasons for being "restless, visionary, and (revolutionary?)." Though they came from different walks of life, they somehow came to the same conclusion about the future. They each thought they could find the solution to their problems in a place called Oregon.

Burnett got the idea when he read about a bill then pending in Congress that proposed to donate land to anyone emigrating to that distant land. As he interpreted it, he could receive 640 acres for himself and 160 acres for each child — a total of sixteen hundred acres. If the bill should pass, the land alone would be worth enough to pay off all his debt. Elated, he called his creditors together and sought their consent to migrate to Oregon. They agreed. "Take what may be necessary for the trip," they said, "leave us what you can spare, and pay us the balance when you can do so."

Land did not interest Jesse Applegate. He already had that. Oregon appealed to him for a more subtle reason. As he wrote:

> *This state of things [the depression] created much discontent and restlessness among a people who had for many generations been nomadic, and had been taught by the example of their ancestors to seek a home in a 'new country' as a sure way of bettering their condition.*

He and his kind were seeking relief by following what he called, "the inherent restlessness of our nature."

Dan Waldo wrote that he first got the idea of going to Oregon when he learned that it was a healthy country. For some time, missionaries and adventurers acquainted with Oregon had been spreading the word about the wholesome climate they had found. For example, there was one tall tale about an emigrant to California who carried ague with him to the promised land and one day came down with the characteristic chills. It was declared that when people heard about it they came from miles around just to watch him shake. They had never seen anything so curious.

And why was Oregon the cure for Jim Nesmith? While reminiscing many years later, he said he found that a difficult question to answer. He had heard a lot about the place, of course, and he was curious, but mostly he had nothing better to do. As he explained, "No tie of near kindred or possessions bound me to any spot on the earth's surface. Thinking my condition might be made better, and knowing it could not be worse, I took the leap in the dark."

Courthouse Square - Independence, Missouri

Curiously, none of the family men were sufficiently sure of themselves to head out alone; each of them organized wagon parties to accompany them. Jesse Applegate had a ready-made following with his two older brothers, Lindsay and Charles, and their families. But many of his St. Clair County, Missouri, neighbors joined them as well. Dan Waldo, one of those neighbors, organized his own train and left one week after Jesse.

Meanwhile, Burnett, in his words, "set to work most vigorously to organize a wagon company. I visited the surrounding counties, making speeches wherever I could find a sufficient audience, and succeeded even beyond my expectations."

It is reported that Burnett was quite the orator. Edward Lenox told of how he and his father had gone to the county seat to hear him speak. They found him atop a soap box outside his store where he was regaling the crowd with the marvels of Oregon:

Then, with a twinkle in his eye he said, 'Gentlemen, they do say, that out in Oregon the pigs are running about under the great acorn trees, round and fat, and already cooked, with knives and forks sticking in them so that you can cut off a slice whenever you are hungry. . . . Now gentlemen, as many of you as would like to go, walk right into my store and put down your names in the book which I have there.

According to Lenox, his father was the first to sign the book.

The Applegate, Waldo, and Burnett trains, along with many others, headed for the same place to embark for Oregon. Without knowledge of each other's plans, they all drove their teams toward Independence, Missouri.

Why Independence? Because, for a good many years it was the only outpost of civilization on the frontier of the United States. Actually, by 1843, it shared the title of "jumping off spot" with a smaller town named Westport (today's Kansas City), which had arisen twelve miles farther west, one mile from the state's western border. But everyone still thought of Independence as the main town. In the words of a contemporary, Josiah Gregg, a noted participant in the trade with Mexico over the Sante Fe trail:

[After 1831] Independence, but twelve miles from the Indian border and two or three south of the Missouri river, being the most eligible point, soon began to take the lead as a place of debarkation, outfit and departure, which, in spite of all opposition, it has ever since maintained. [He was writing this in 1843.] It is to this beautiful spot, already grown to be a thriving town, that the prairie adventurer, whether in search of wealth, health or amusement, is latterly in the habit of repairing, about the first of May, as the caravans usually set out some time during that month. Here they purchase their provisions for the road, and many of their mules, oxen, and even some of their wagons — in short, load all their vehicles, and make their final preparations for a long journey across the prairie wilderness.

5

Location, location, location as they say in real estate. Of course, experience had something to do with it as well. Ever since the town's founding in 1827 its merchants had been perfecting the business of outfitting wagon caravans. The prairie traveler could expect to find anything there he might need in the way of supplies. As Gregg further stated, "During the season of departure, therefore, it is a place of much bustle and active business."

Certainly that was true in May of 1843. Not only were there several wagons trains of emigrants either already arrived or headed that way but there were also several non-emigrant groups outfitting as well. John Charles Frémont, for instance, was preparing to head west with a government surveying party; Sir William Drummond Stewart of Scotland was in the process of putting together a hunting party of some sixty men for a grand adventure in the Far West; and there was the normal complement of commercial caravans readying to embark upon their annual trek to Sante Fe.

(Frémont and Stewart would have further contact with the Oregon emigrants along the trail and we will have more to say of them at that time.) The point is, Independence and nearby Westport were experiencing more bustle and activity than either had ever before known. The emigrants made the difference. Almost every night new encampments would spring up like mushrooms in the groves and clearings between and around the towns.

One adventurer traveling with the Frémont party described Westport as, "too much like all small villages to need any particular description." Yet, he found shopping for supplies difficult "owing to the great number outfitting," and remarked that the town presented "a lively scene from the number and heterogeneous description of those thronging its narrow streets."

A newspaper correspondent assigned to cover Sir William Stewart's western adventure wrote that he found it "a constant source of interest" to see so many people gathering. One Sunday morning he found himself a spectator as:

. . . five or six wagons passed through the town of Westport,

and one old man with silver hair was with the party. Women and children were walking, fathers and brothers were driving loose cattle or managing the heavy teams, and keen-eyed youngsters, with their chins yet smooth and rifles on their shoulders, kept in advance of the wagons with long strides, looking as if they were already watching around the corners of the streets for game.

In addition, he noted, "Many other small bodies of these adventurous travelers crossed our notice at Independence, Westport, and at encampments made in the vicinity."

The campers and "adventurous travelers" he saw probably included the Burnett and Applegate parties. Missourians such as them constituted the largest number of soon-to-be emigrants. But trains streamed in from all parts of the western country, including Arkansas, Illinois, Kentucky, and Iowa Territory. Peculiarly, as James Nesmith would later write, they arrived as "strangers to one another" and independent, "without orders from any quarter, and without preconcert, promptly as the grass began to start."

Like Applegate, Waldo, Burnett, and Nesmith, each family or individual had personal reasons for coming to the Independence and Westport area. But from now on it would not matter so much why they had come as each of them would be sharing a common goal: they all desired to emigrate to Oregon.

II

In the spring of 1843 the whole western frontier found itself in a state of considerable agitation over the possibilities of a place very few knew anything about. It seemed as though everyone with the slightest itch to move had turned their sights towards the Far West. As a contemporary frontier newspaper expressed it:

The Oregon fever is raging in almost every part of the Union. Companies are forming in the East, and in several parts of

7

Ohio, which, added to those of Illinois, Iowa, and Missouri, will make a pretty formidable army. . . . It would be reasonable to suppose that there will be at least five thousand Americans west of the Rocky Mountains by next autumn.

Five thousand? To put that number in some kind of perspective, consider that, at the time, there were scarcely more than two or three hundred Americans in the entire Pacific Northwest. Actually the newspaper observer grossly over-estimated the number that would move that year; numbers that large would not occur for some time yet. But the nearly nine-hundred that did head west in the 1843 train exceeded anything that had occurred before by such a large margin that it has been known ever since as the Great Migration.

Many volumes have been produced about the Oregon Trail experience over the years; yet, it is still hard to appreciate what these people were setting out to accomplish. In truth, nothing of that scope had ever before been attempted. No emigrant wagon had yet traveled all the way to the Columbia River from the United States frontier. Jesse Applegate modestly expressed it this way: "The migration of a large body of men, women and children across the continent to Oregon, was, in the year 1843, strictly an experiment." Experiment indeed. It was a huge gamble!

Horace Greeley, a nationally respected editor, looked at what they planned and cried:

For what do they brave the desert, the wilderness, the savage, the snowy precipices of the Rocky Mountains, the weary summer march, the storm-drenched bivouac and the gnawing of famine? — This migration . . . to Oregon wears an aspect of insanity.

Perhaps it was insane, Applegate himself admitted to being afflicted with a "species of madness" in making such a decision. Yet, even had the effort failed it would never have been forgotten.

Several hundred independent American citizens had arrived at a major crossroad in their lives at the same point in history. To satisfy their dreams they were willing to accept the risk of being branded as fools or mourned as martyrs. But, regardless, come what may, they were going to Oregon. Though engaged in "strictly an experiment," to their everlasting renown the experiment worked. Instead of laughing stock they became the inspiration and precursor for a flood tide of humanity that, following in their wake, changed the history and composition of the United States for all time.

To complicate matters in 1843, the country they aimed for did not belong exclusively to the Americans. Oregon, comprising all the territory above the 42nd parallel (today's existing state line between Oregon and California) between the crest of the Rockies and the Pacific Ocean up to today's southern border of Alaska, had been disputed land since its discovery. By the mid-nineteenth century, however, only two nations remained in contention for ultimate sovereignty — Great Britain and the United States.

Neither contender claimed all of the territory but they could not agree upon a boundary between themselves. Great Britain wanted to draw a line along the Columbia River up to 49 degrees with everything north and west of there going to them. The United States, on the other hand, insisted upon extending the existing boundary between Canada and themselves, the 49th parallel, all the way to the Pacific. (The crux of the dispute, then, amounted to a large percentage of the land now comprising the state of Washington.) Despite several frustrating attempts at resolution, the best that could be agreed upon amounted to a stalemate. By virtue of a treaty signed in 1818, and renewed for an indefinite period in 1827, each granted the other the right to what they termed "joint occupation" of all of the territory.

Beginning shortly after the signing of the 1818 treaty there were several attempts to stir up interest in Oregon among Americans but none of the efforts succeeded. As a result, for several years the joint occupancy agreement worked to benefit only the

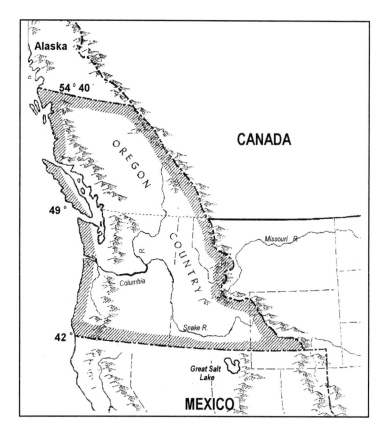

British fur-traders and trappers already operating extensively in the area.

From the mid-1830's on, however, American missionaries began moving into the country and their labors among the various Indian tribes resulted in information filtering back to the states that inadvertently excited interest among many farmers on the frontier. A close reading of the reports published in various religious journals and newspapers of the time revealed that while the Oregon missions were finding it difficult to turn heathens into Christians, they were achieving considerable success in teaching them to farm.

The land of the Willamette Valley, especially, had proven exceedingly fruitful. The climate was mild, rainfall abundant, and access to markets handy. The more the discontented among the frontier population heard about the place, the better it began to look. And eventually, as we have seen, it was an accumulation of discontents, not a place in history, that drove the majority of would-be emigrants to Independence in 1843.

III

As the nation's restless began casting their eyes longingly towards Oregon as the solution to their problems, they were merely reflecting their heritage. Americans had been moving west for generations. It was in their blood. It mattered little that Great Britain and the United States still debated final boundaries in the Pacific Northwest. Restless pioneers, or squatters, seldom concerned themselves with political considerations. Homes were what they cared about, especially homes and opportunities in unsettled lands. Ever since the colonial days of King George such people had been a thorn in the side of law-makers.

And it was not just the English Parliament that attempted to control settlement. After America's separation from England, Congress moved quickly to curb land-hungry frontiersmen. They enacted laws making it illegal to settle on land until it had been surveyed; they insisted upon respect for Indian rights until relinquished by treaty; and they decreed that frontier lands could be acquired only by purchase on the open market. Yet pioneers continually ignored such legalities. They pushed out into the unoccupied country anyway, always hoping the next place they landed would be better than the one they were leaving. And they knew from experience that once enough of them had settled in a given place the government would knuckle under and make it legal.

The generation maturing in the mid-nineteenth century, however, had for years believed that the old pioneering adventures would never be available to them. They were living on what most observers conceded was the last frontier.

The land beyond Missouri had been written off as worthless for farming; trees would not grow there and if trees would not grow neither would crops. So went the thinking of the time. They branded the land, "The Great American Desert," and forgot it. Now, though, they were hearing about a land that seemed to have considerable value; it had plenty of trees, more than enough water, and a nearby market. The old itch returned. For many all it took to relieve it was the action of a Missouri senator named Linn.

Late in 1841 Dr. Lewis Linn created quite a stir when he began pressing Congress to encourage emigration to Oregon by donating land to those who would settle there. He and his colleague, the senior senator from Missouri, Thomas Benton, had long been advocates of western expansion. They wanted to see the stalemate with England broken in the United States' favor and believed the best way to accomplish it was through settlement. But, as Tom Benton declared, "nobody will go three thousand miles to settle a new country, unless he gets land by it."

Free government land was unheard of in the mid-nineteenth century though pioneers had been crying for it for generations. They argued that the government should not sell its vacant lands, it should grant them as a reward to those willing to undergo the risks and hardships of settling on the nation's frontiers. This appeal had been made by frontiersmen since Revolutionary War days, but Congress had always been unresponsive. Now though, there was new cause for hope. If the Linn bill should pass they would have their way at last — at least in Oregon.

Dr. Linn proposed his bill in December, 1841 and labored fourteen months to bring it to a favorable vote in the Senate. The opposition, led by South Carolina senators Calhoun and McDuffie, worried that passage of the bill would violate the existing joint occupation treaty, thus proving an affront to England and threaten war. Further, McDuffie considered Oregon not worth the effort. In his speech against the bill he stated, "Why, sir, of what use will this be for agricultural purposes? I would not for that purpose give a pinch of snuff for the whole territory."

The arguments of the opposition were attacked head-on in a splendid rebuttal of McDuffie's speech by Dr. Linn:

> *The senator from South Carolina some what inconsistently urges that the country is bleak, barren, volcanic, rocky, a waste always flooded when it is not parched; and insists that, worthless as it is, Great Britain will go at once to war for it. Strange that she should in 1818 have held so tenaciously to what is so worthless! Stranger still, that she should have stuck yet closer to it in 1827, when she had still ampler time to learn the bootlessness of the possession! And strangest of all that she should still cling to it with the grasp of death! Sir, I cannot for my life help thinking that she and the senator have formed a very different estimate of the territory, and that she is (as she ought to be) a good deal better informed.*

Dr. Linn proved the more persuasive orator. On February 3, 1843 the Senate passed the bill by a vote of 24-22. The next hurdle stood in the House of Representatives.

It was about this time that Peter Burnett learned of the bill and saw it as a way of paying his debts. As noted, since he felt "there was a fair prospect of the ultimate passage of the bill," he organized a wagon company. One of his recruits, twenty-eight year old Ninevah Ford, spoke for many when he said, "One proud object we had was the prospect of obtaining a donation of land if the country was worth staying in."

So, as congress debated the wisdom of encouraging American settlement in the disputed Oregon country, farm folks of the western frontier, such as Burnett and his followers, decided that the passage of the bill by the Senate was all the encouragement they needed. One observer wrote; "this is the proper way to "take possession" of Oregon. Individual enterprise, these days, is everything — government protection to private speculation worse than nothing."

The lethargy brought on by the long depression had run its course. American blood was boiling again. "WHOO HA!" they cried, "Go it boys! We're in a perfect Oregon Fever!"

CHAPTER TWO

Preparing to Go

I

I t may not be immediately obvious but one of the characteristics of the Oregon migration experience that set it apart from previous such movements (besides the extraordinary distance traveled) was that the trip effectively required a wagon.

Earlier Americans generally had the option of rafting down a river to the new frontier. In fact, from the time the first pioneers crossed the Appalachians the rivers had functioned as the major highways of the westering experience. Now though, after crossing the Mississippi, the rivers flowed east out of the Rockies, just the opposite of the way emigrants wanted to go. In addition, there were no large navigable rivers like the Ohio or Tennessee that could safely accommodate a steamboat for part of the distance.

Of course, they could have used a pack train of mules. The fur trading companies had done so for years in moving out into the foothills of the Rockies for their annual rendezvous. A pack train was a faster means of transportation than a wagon — it would cut at least one month off the travel time — and fording streams and crossing rough terrain would be much easier.

But the use of mules presented some problems as well. For one thing, the packs the animals bore would have to be removed every night and reloaded every morning. That was no simple task. In the fur-trade they declared that loading required, "the patience of Job, the strength of Samson, and the wisdom of Solomon." (The nasty job was therefore assigned to the newest recruits.)

John Boardman of the 1843 train was a young man traveling without the encumbrance of family and he did use a pack mule.

He learned early what he was in for. On his second day out from Missouri he wrote, "My mule laid down and got his load off and in a short time ran away and broke his crupper. Soon got loose again, but no damage; did not appear to like packing."

Many men who used mules on long trips grumbled that they soon became little more than a slave to their animals. With such an attitude, it is not surprising that considerable hard-feelings often developed between man and beast. During the gold-rush years pack trains of mules did become more prevalent since the California-bound argonauts were almost all men in great haste. But the emigration to Oregon would be a family movement and mules were hardly the reasonable choice for men who had their wives and children with them.

The Oregon wagon-trains always consisted of many small children, mothers with infants, pregnant women, the infirm, and the elderly. It would have been a terrible hardship to expect them to ride horses or mules all the way. Besides, in a mule train there was no effective way of providing passage for the sick or injured if such calamity should befall the family on the trip. So, it was no accident that "the house on wheels," the white-topped wagon, grew to become the symbol of the Oregon Trail.

Since a wagon proved to be the reasonable choice, what kind of wagon was best? This is a source of one of the great misconceptions about the Oregon travelers. Ask anyone what kind of wagon comes to mind when you mention the Trail and most of the time you will hear, "the Conestoga." But such was not the case. The Conestoga developed out of the necessities for movement east of the Mississippi where the distances were far shorter and there were at least primitive roads to follow. It also came into prominence along the Sante Fe Trail for use in the commercial caravans to Mexico, again for a much shorter distance and over smoother terrain than that facing the Oregon emigrants.

The chief problem with the Conestoga for the Oregon-bound was its tremendous bulk. An attempt to move such a heavy vehicle over the vast plains, across rivers, and through mountainous terrain would have added a whole new dimension to the hardships encountered — and probably would have killed the team before they got half way.

If not the Conestoga, then what? In the early years the wagon of choice became the simple farm wagon. The majority of the emigrants were farmers anyway and already had one or more such vehicles. They needed a well-made wagon, however, one strong enough to hold together on a long, arduous trip. Yet it also had to be light enough that the draught animals could pull it all the way without killing themselves. Strong but light, incompatible features that demanded a compromise.

Jesse Looney of the '43 train wrote back to his brother after reaching Oregon, "you cannot be too particular in choice of a wagon. It should be strong in every part and yet it should not be very heavy." Peter Burnett agreed, "Beware of heavy wagons, as they break down your teams for no purpose, and you will not need them."

In selecting a wagon there were three parts to consider: the bed, the top and the running gear. The bed was generally quite simple. It consisted of a rectangular box about 9-10 feet long by 4 feet wide with sides 2 to 2 1/2 feet high. Most were straight-sided but Peter Burnett recommended having the topmost section bevel out to avoid the possibility of water running down from the canvas top and entering the wagon. In addition, some families traveled with a wagon-bed that contained a false bottom. Beneath it they would store the items they would not require until the end of the journey, such as farm tools and implements, for example.

Seasoned hard woods made the best material for wagon beds. Boards of oak, hickory, or maple provided tight seams that could be sealed with caulking. '43 emigrant S. M. Gilmore explained the importance of that feature, "Have your wagon beds made in such a manner that they can be used for boats; you will find them of great service in crossing streams."

The next part of the wagon, the top, gave the least problems while providing an important function. Gilmore advised, "have your wagons well covered, so that they will not leak, or your provisions and clothes will spoil." Thus, the famous white top. It was usually of canvas or waterproofed material (and not always white, though Burnett warned against painting the fabric as that could cause it to crack) supported by bows of bent hickory that provided for 5-6 feet of head-room down the middle of an empty wagon. Most tops had flaps at the front and puckering strings at back for both privacy and ventilation. About the worst that could happen to the top would be to tear it. But, since there were few trees on the prairie, that seldom happened. A windstorm could create havoc though, sometimes requiring temporary removal of the top to prevent tip-overs.

The running gear was far and away the most important consideration in choosing a good wagon. It was almost always the running gear that gave the most problems. Tongues snapped on sharp turns or drops, axles broke, and wheels shrank in the heat. Unfortunately, carrying along spare parts presented a problem because of weight and space limitations. Though some emigrants did carry a large piece of unfinished timber suspended beneath their wagon, most of the time repairs had to be made from materials available in the wild. That could be a severe handicap on the prairie where the nearest tree might be a couple days ride away.

Wheels were the most critical part of the running gear. They were the one item that could be considered irreplaceable. If a wheel broke, forget it. About the best an emigrant could do under that circumstance would be to cut his four-wheel wagon down to a two-wheel cart. Little wonder teamsters spent so much time worrying about keeping the running gear in good shape.

The selection of a wagon, then, came down to a few basics. But the motive power, that was another story altogether! When it came time to decide upon the team to draw the emigrant across the plains, there were three choices: horses, mules, or oxen. Yet the debate over which was best never ended.

The horse made the most sense to a farmer. Most of them took pride in their teams and to part with them could be like losing one of the family. Yet in the Independence\Westport area they heard the old-timers declare that horses did not have the stamina to pull a wagon all the way to Oregon. Horses needed grain and good forage, they said, but grain was too heavy to carry and forage along the trail would be sparse. Horses could serve as saddle animals all right, but not to pull the wagon. Further, even those horses taken along to ride required constant guarding because the Indians loved to steal horses.

As for mules, they had been used for years by the Sante Fe traders in moving their heavy wagons to Mexico and back. Those men had learned by experience that a mule could withstand heat, poor forage, and poor shelter better than a horse. In addition, they found mules less likely to overdrink or overeat and less susceptible to digestive disorders. They were fast and strong and Indians seldom attempted to steal them. Unfortunately, they had a down side as well. Breaking a mule to harness could be extremely trying to say the least.

Josiah Gregg, the Santa Fe trader, wrote, "The . . . great difficulty the traders have to encounter is in training those animals that have never before been worked, which is frequently attended by an immensity of trouble." He might have added without fear of contradiction that even when broken they remained the most intractable of animals.

To add to the woes, mules were quite susceptible to straying. If the animal got loose at night it could be difficult to find and, if found, difficult to get back to camp. John Boardman, the 1843 diarist who used mules, made frequent reference to the long-eared darlings. For instance:

Yesterday 3 of Chiles' mules ran away.

A hailstorm . . . drove our mules away.

After trying for one week in vain to catch my mule, we drove him into a pen here [at Fort Laramie] and caught him with a rope.

Mules ran off with packs; too dark to find them.

Made a good day's travel. A run after mules.

Little wonder that along the western overland trails teamsters wasted more profanity on mules than any other single irritation.

So, what about the ox? This docile creature had many features to admire. Though the slowest of all the choices (top speed, two to three miles per hour), they were also the easiest to handle. They had more stamina and could subsist on poorer forage than either the horse or the mule. They seldom strayed and if they did they were easy to lead back to camp. Like the mule, the threat of theft by Indians was minimal, and they were cheaper than mules by a ratio of least 3 to 1. (In 1843 an ox would cost about $25 while a mule would go for $75 to $100.)

As an added plus, though many hesitated to think about it, in a dire emergency you could eat the ox. You could eat the mule too, of course, mountain-men did it frequently (they would eat anything, for, as they expressed it, "meat is meat."), but most farm families considered eating mules or horses taboo.

Peter Burnett wrote back to the states immediately after reaching Oregon to inform future emigrants how to prepare for the trip and what to expect along the way. He had this to say about the choice of draft animals:

> *We fully tested the ox and mule teams, and we found the ox teams greatly superior. One ox will pull as much as two mules, and, in mud, as much as four. They are more easily managed, are not so subject to be lost or broken down on the way, cost less at the start, and are worth about four times as much here. The ox is a most noble animal, patient, thrifty, durable, gentle, and easily driven, and does not run off. Those who come to this country will be in love with their oxen by the time they reach here.*

Equally convincing was a letter written about the same time by '43 emigrant, S. M. Gilmore, who also meant to provide guidance to later emigrants. He said:

> *Though I wrote while on the Sweetwater that mule teams were preferable, but after seeing them thoroughly tried I have become convinced that oxen are more preferable — they are the least trouble and stand traveling much the best — are worth a great deal more when here.*

So, in the early years, the popular configuration became just what Gilmore described in his letter, "Your wagons should be light, yet substantial and strong, and a plenty of good oxen."

How many oxen did you need? According to Gilmore, "Load your wagons light and put one third more team to them than is necessary to pull the load." Jesse Looney's ratio was greater, "Put in as much loading as one yoke of cattle can draw handily, and then put on three good yoke of cattle and take an extra yoke for change in case of failure from lameness or sore necks."

The records show that most emigrants used three yoke (pairs) of oxen though four would not be uncommon.

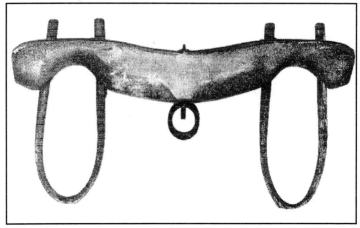

The yoke, incidentally, was simply a heavy bar of wood about four feet long that contained two U-shaped, round hickory bows. The bows, about an inch to an inch and a half in diameter, slipped in and out of holes bored through the bar. Once the ox's head was in place, the bow was secured with a wooden pin or metal bolt at the point where it poked through the top of the bar. A metal ring dangling from the center of the bar was connected to the wagon tongue or to a chain that served as an extension of the tongue. The ox's shoulders then pushed against the yoke to move the wagon. There was no harness.

What about the loading, as Looney called it? That, too, was a subject of much concern around the camp fires outside of Independence. They could not be sure what to carry in 1843. By the time they arrived in Oregon, however, Burnett had learned one lesson that many of the emigrants had ignored to their regret, "The loading should consist of mostly provisions." Do not bring furniture, he warned, and then added:

All heavy articles should be left, except a few cooking vessels, one shovel, and a pair of pot hooks. Clothes enough to last a year, and several pair of strong, heavy shoes to each person, it will be well to bring. If you are heavily loaded let the quantity of sugar and coffee be small, as milk is preferable and does not have to be hauled. You should take a water keg, and a few tin cups, tin plates, tin saucers, and butcher knives; and there should be a small grindstone in company as the tools become dull on the way.

Gilmore recommended, "You should bring about 200 pounds of flour, 100 pounds of bacon, for every member of the family that can eat, besides other provisions. . . . You will find some beans, rice and dried fruit of great use on the road." He also added as an after-thought, "You will find some ship biscuit to be of great use at times when you can not find fuel sufficient to cook with."

After a few years, guide-books advised that a family of four should carry about 800 pounds of flour, 200 pounds of lard, 700 pounds of bacon, 200 pounds of beans, 100 pounds of dried fruit, 75 pounds of coffee, and 25 pounds of salt and pepper. One popular book recommended that because of the physical demands of the trip a family should take twice as much food as they would expect to consume in a like amount of time at home.

Most of the early emigrant companies believed they would supplement their food supply by hunting and fishing along the way, but they soon found that impractical. Both Looney and Gilmore warned against depending upon it. Looney, for instance, wrote his brother, "I cannot urge you too strongly to be sure to bring plenty of provisions; don't depend on the game you may get. You may get some and you may not. It is uncertain." Gilmore stated bluntly, "Make no calculations on getting buffalo or other wild meat, for you are only wasting your time and killing horses and mules to get it."

Loading then was the source of some anxiety (and undoubtedly some arguments). In addition to provisions, the emigrant needed room for tools, cooking utensils, guns and ammunition, private baggage, spare parts, and maybe an heirloom or two that simply could not be left behind. Unless the family could afford several wagons, some tough decisions were required. They dared not overload. Gilmore warned, "if you overload you will lose your team, wagon and goods."

Unfortunately, many times it was only after the teams began to wear down that the overloading became apparent. Over the years many a fine piece of furniture found a new resting place on the prairie between Missouri and today's state of Nebraska as testimony to misjudgment or ignorance on departure day.

As these discussions have revealed, the trip to Oregon was not cheap. Assuming only one wagon (and many had more than that), it could cost between $300-$600 for a team and wagon, another like amount for supplies, plus some funds to set up a home in the Far-West. Assume an average of about $1000. That was a lot of money at a time when $1.00 a day was considered good wages.

What this points out is that the migration to Oregon was essentially a middle-class movement. The rich had no reason to go and the poor could not afford it. That does not mean that representatives from those class extremes did not go, it simply means they were the exceptions. One way poor people did make the trip, incidentally, was as employees of the more well-to-do. A large number of young people without means earned their way to the Pacific coast as teamsters, cooks, or baby-sitters.

II

In mid-May the day finally arrived when the 1843 emigrants believed they could quit haggling over supplies and equipment and begin the actual migration. But wiser heads prevailed long enough to convince almost everyone that one additional item of business had to be dealt with. With nearly a thousand people and more than 120 wagons, they had to get organized. Accordingly, on the 17th of May posters circulated through the various encampments inviting all who planned to make the trip to Oregon to meet the next day.

The meeting took place at a spot known as Fitzhugh's Mill. Committees were formed to draw up rules for the journey and to check out the equipment of the various emigrants to assure their adequate preparation. Two days later a written agreement, with the avowed purpose, "of keeping good order and promoting civil and military discipline," received approval. The document revealed a lot about the emigrants of that year.

They were democratic — every male over the age of sixteen would be entitled to a vote in all affairs of the company; they lived in an age when most adult men had served time in their local militia so they were familiar with the demands of the military — they decreed that every man with the vote could expect to take his turn at guard duty; they were cautious about granting authority — they would elect officers only after a shakedown period in which they could get to know each other better. (They scheduled the elections to occur when the train reached the Kansas River.)

In addition, they provided for the recall of elected officials whenever 1/3 of the company called for a new election. Finally, they agreed to elect a council of nine to function as judge and jury in the settlement of disputes within the company. It was not necessary for them to specify that the government of the Company was strictly a male concern (at least on the surface). In strict accordance with mid-nineteenth century standards, that was understood. Without further debate, on Saturday, May 20, 1843, the Oregon Emigrating Company was born; departure date was set for the following Monday.

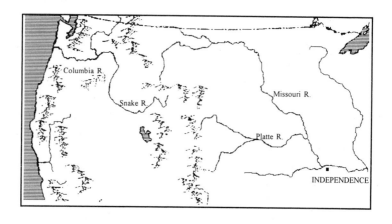

CHAPTER THREE

The Epic Journey Begins

Week 1: May 21 - May 27

W ith an organizational scheme in place, the emigrant leaders appointed a special committee to secure the services of a guide. Since no one in the train knew the way to Oregon, and no maps existed to assist them, this was a mission of considerable importance. Fortunately it did not prove too difficult since there happened to be several men in the vicinity with just the knowledge required. They were known as Rocky Mountain fur trappers.

Ever since the Lewis and Clark expedition of 1804-06 had revealed the extraordinary beaver harvest available in Far-West streams, the Rocky Mountain fur trade had been the training ground for a group of hardy frontiersmen known collectively as Mountain Men. In their single-minded pursuit of beaver pelts, such men as Jedediah Smith, Jim Bridger, Thomas Fitzpatrick, Kit Carson, Joe Meek, and others won undying fame as they scoured every inch of the territory between the settlements in Missouri and the lava plains of the Snake River plateau in today's Idaho. Some, such as Smith, even blazed trails into the modern states of California and Oregon.

Their's was a risky, demanding, and often savage life that took a tremendous toll upon its practitioners; some have estimated the mortality rate in the profession to be as high as 75%. But by 1843 the business was dying out. Silk had replaced beaver as the fashion choice in hats and many former trappers found they could no longer make a living in the old ways. They still had invaluable knowledge about the routes west though. And that was exactly what the Oregon Emigrating Company needed.

The 1843 emigrants chose John Gantt, age fifty-three, as their guide. It is likely his background had impressed them. He had once served in the United States Army, attaining the rank of Captain, (that was how he was known — Captain Gantt) and from the time he left the Army in 1829 he had made his living in the fur trade. He was accustomed to the responsibilities of command and he knew the territory.

Jesse Applegate described him as, "a borderer who has passed his life on the verge of civilization and has been chosen to the post of leader from his knowledge of the savage and his experience in travel through roadless wastes." Though Jesse did not mention it, the Captain had one other important qualification — he was unemployed. Doubtless the emigrants of 1843 had little difficulty in persuading him to guide them as far as Fort Hall for a fee of one dollar per head.

Fort Hall, in what is now the state of Idaho, was as far west as most of the American mountain men had traveled, including Gantt. Ordinarily that would have been a serious problem since once they reached the fort the emigrants would still be faced with a journey of some seven hundred miles to the Willamette Valley, but the leaders were not concerned. They had already met with a man who knew that portion of the route well, and he had agreed to join them en route. His name was Marcus Whitman.

Whitman had lived in the Far West since 1836, employed as a missionary doctor by the Presbyterians. His assigned station in the Oregon Country was near the Hudson's Bay post of Fort Walla Walla on the Columbia River. He happened to be passing through Independence on his way back to his post when approached by the emigrants. As we shall see, that coincidence proved a benefit to each party.

II

On Sunday, May 21, as the emigrants began rolling their wagons out of various camps towards the agreed-upon departure point beyond the state line, they were, for all they knew, leaving the United States forever. Twenty-two year old diarist Jim Nesmith might have had that in mind as he wrote, "This day was fine and clear. Took a farewell look at the State of Missouri." Another young bachelor, Pierson Reading, also revealed a tinge of feeling as he recorded, "We have now bid farewell to the home of the 'Pale faces.'"

This is an aspect of the overland journey that is difficult for moderns to appreciate. Today, there is no place on earth that could not be reached in a few days if necessary. Yet these people were setting out for a goal that would require a journey of at least six months without any options available to reduce that time by more than a month. With such a prospect in sight, most of them had no thought of ever returning. It is understandable, then, that some looked back with a tinge of remorse. Not everyone left on this great adventure with the same amount of enthusiasm anyway. Especially not the women.

Though no women's diaries of the 1843 experience have ever come to light, surely many of them shared the feelings of later females who did record their thoughts. One historian who studied sex roles in the overland migrations wrote, "In their diaries and recollections many women discussed the way in which the decision to move was made. Not one wife initiated the idea; it was always the husband." Further, he said, of those who discussed the issue, less than one-fourth agreed with the decision while nearly one-third said they moved only reluctantly. Another historian agreed. As a result of her own studies she could state, "the period of Overland Trail migration (1840-1860) produces overwhelming evidence that women did not greet the idea of going West with enthusiasm."

Even though evidence available for the women's story in the 1843 migration is meager, we can determine this: Peter Burnett wrote of asking permission of his creditors to go west, he did not mention asking his wife. He did record, though, that her physicians said, "the trip would either kill or cure her." It would be interesting to know what she felt about that. Daniel Waldo later said of the Oregon trip, "I did not come here to make money; I just came for my health." He did not say why his wife came.

The closest we can come to determining a wife's motive is circumstantial at best. For instance, the editor of William Newby's diary included this statement in his introduction, "Tales of rich lands and mild climate of the Oregon Territory kindled in Newby the desire to emigrate to the Pacific Coast, while the death of two of Mrs. Newby's brothers, only a day apart in September, 1842, doubtless hastened the decision to leave." From this it might be supposed that sorrow "kindled **her** desire to emigrate."

One woman, Sarah Owens, age twenty-five, had just given birth in February. How do you suppose she felt about undertaking such a trip with three children, the youngest of whom was not yet four months old? Sara Jane Hill, age nineteen, had just lost her first child. Was she looking for escape? Also, she and several other women were pregnant when the train left Missouri. (Jesse Looney wrote in October, 1843, "there were some eight to ten births" on the trail.) It might be expected that ladies in such a condition would have left civilization with some concern about the prospects of delivering a child in the wilderness.

It seems, then, that the long journey probably began for many families in a less than congenial atmosphere. Besides, the departure had been delayed beyond what the leaders had hoped for because of a late spring and short grass.

The grass had been the key. Adequate forage was absolutely necessary; the teams had to eat. The problem with waiting too long, however, was the risk of encountering an early winter at the western end of the journey. Since no one knew for certain how long the trip would take, the timing of departure day was the cause of more than a little anxiety.

III

The afternoon of Monday, May 22nd, found most of the Company encamped at a spot thirty-five miles from Independence called Elm Grove. Two elm trees and some dogwood bushes comprised the grove. The Sante Fe traders had left the larger of the two elms in sad shape after having chopped it up for fuel. Still, Peter Burnett found it a beautiful place (although he observed that he learned here for the first time that two trees could constitute a grove). Many of the emigrants were in high spirits that evening, he said, glad to be underway at last. He later recalled the picture:

No scene appeared to our enthusiastic vision more exquisite than the sight of so many wagons, tents, fires, cattle, and people, as were here collected. At night the sound of joyous music was heard in the tents. Our long journey thus began in sunshine and song, in anecdote and laughter; but these all vanished before we reached its termination.

Burnett's happy camp scene underscores a persistent pattern of the early migrations — the emigrants were almost totally ignorant of what lay ahead of them. That was probably just as well. Many of them might never have gone if they had known how hard the trip would be.

Two days beyond Elm Grove, about twenty-two miles, the train faced its first difficult river crossing. Western men of those days had considerable experience in crossing rivers with wagons as there were few bridges on the frontier, but normally the route had been broken long before by others. Now they found themselves as the road-makers.

This stream, the Wakarusa, was nothing out of the ordinary but it did have high, steep banks that required easing the wagons down at the end of a tether. This was accomplished by tying ropes to the rear axles of the wagons and then allowing them to roll gently down the bank as several men played out the line. The teamster then drove to the opposite shore where, if necessary, teams of oxen were added to his own to pull his wagon up the 45-degree bank. Later, to their consternation, the 1843 emigrants learned that a much more practicable ford existed across the Wakarusa about 100 yards above where they labored.

During the evening of May 24th, a Wednesday, Captain Gantt joined the train and assumed his duties as guide. On the 25th, recorded Pierson Reading, the train camped on both sides of, "a small creek with good water and sufficient wood for fire. Delightful weather." The next day the initial wagons arrived at what would prove to be the first big test, the Kansas River.

Spring rains had swollen the Kansas to the point that it was what Reading called "swimming." Fording was out of the question. A committee of three tried to hire a platform from a Frenchman named Papin who lived near the crossing but they found his demands unreasonable. So, they decided to build a ferry of their own. As that work progressed, another group of emigrants, unwilling to wait any longer, made their own arrangement with Papin and began crossing. As Peter Burnett remembered it, "this produced great dissatisfaction in camp."

Thus surfaced for the first time the problem the emigrants would face all the way to Oregon. The Company consisted of fiercely independent individuals forced together, in Burnett's words, in "a new and trying position." There would be "ten

31

thousand little vexations continually recurring" he said, that often brought out "the worst traits of human nature." For instance, on the way to the Kansas, he noted in disgust, emigrants raced for position without regard for their teams or their neighbors though they had nearly two thousand miles to go.

Obviously the Company needed to come together, but they had earlier agreed to wait until after crossing the Kansas River to set up their official organization. There was little to do now but proceed as planned.

As fortune would have it, those unhappy with the splinter group that had hired Papin's platform had an opportunity to gloat when that conveyance sank. Luckily, though some property was lost, no one drowned. Sara Jane Hill, a young woman at the time, later remembered the incident well:

> *During the crossing, when it came to old man Zachary's turn he loaded [the] boat too heavy, they tried to keep him from it, but could not. Then he put two of his daughters on top of the load [plus two other women]. Near the middle of the stream it capsized, turned everything out, two big Indians threw their blankets, jumped in and rescued the girls. This was done for free but they had to be paid to bring out the provisions.*

The ferry constructed by the remainder of the company consisted of round poles laid between two dugout canoes. They rolled their wagons onto the platform one at a time and ferried them across by tugging on long ropes attached to each end of the raft. After unloading the wagon on the other side of the river, they would then pull the raft back and repeat the whole process. They had to do this for more than 100 wagons. Not surprisingly, Pierson Reading described it as "a very tedious process."

While the ferrying continued, several men swam the river to help guide the raft or to move the animals. Pleasant Kaiser, age fifteen at the time, would later remember such crossings fondly.

Forty-five years later he said, "to me it was great sport to be in the water and swimming around." (He seems to have lived up to his given name.)

Not everyone had such fond recollections, however. Take William Vaughn for example. In the midst of leading some stock across the Kansas, he suddenly suffered an attack of the cramps. Fortunately, Jim Nesmith happened to be in the water and saw his plight. Quickly, Jim swam to the rescue only to find himself in the clutches of a desperate and frantic young man. Struggle as he might he could not free himself or save Vaughn; he began to fear he too would drown until he received the aid of another man named Stewart.

The two men finally succeeded in subduing the drowning youngster and getting him to shore, though by the time they did he had lapsed into unconsciousness. An alert teen-age observer, Edward Lenox, rushed to his father's wagon for a keg and Nesmith and Stewart laid the limp Vaughn over it and began pumping his arms in an attempt to revive him. Finally, as they were near giving up, signs of life returned. After some warm coffee and rest, he came around completely. And, according to Lenox, "on the second day he was able to take his place again."

The capsized raft and Vaughn's frightening experience served to warn everyone of the danger of river crossings. Over the years many would lose their lives in situations similar to these. So far the 1843 emigrants had been lucky, but then, they had only just begun.

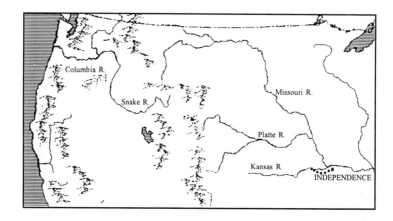

CHAPTER FOUR

The Moving Community

Week Two: May 28 - June 3

T he Oregon Emigrating Company spent six exhausting days crossing the Kansas River. They were nine days into their journey and had traveled fifty-five miles from Elm Grove; no one needed reminding now of the necessity of keeping the train moving if they expected to reach their destination before winter set in.

The families that crossed the river first set up camp while waiting for the rest of the Company. It was too early in the journey to enjoy the idleness and time dragged for those not actually employed in the crossing. They called the site Camp Delay.

Pierson Reading used his leisure time to write to some of his relatives and friends since, he said, a French trader happened to be passing through on his way to the settlements. Eleven days later, another emigrant of 1843, M. M. McCarver, used the same type of delivery service for a letter dated June 10, as he explained it, "The return of a company of mountain traders to the settlements presents an opportunity for writing which I feel much inclined to embrace." A letter-writer in Frémont's expeditionary force, William Gilpin, sent a message back to the states dated July 26, 1843, that began as follows, "I drop you a line by a couple of Shawnee Indians, who are going to Missouri from this place."

These examples show how travelers in the Far West maintained communications with friends and family back in civilization. They also show how trusting people were when it came to delivery of their mail. Without hesitation they asked perfect strangers who happened to be going in the right direction to carry their letters back to the states. There is considerable evidence to suggest that their confidence in others was seldom misplaced.

While at Camp Delay, the emigrants not only wrote letters but also received several visits from the local Indian tribe, the Kanzas (or Kaws). They were not enchanted. Reading found the natives to be, "miserable wretches, begging for food and stealing all they can lay their hands on." The delightful diarist William Newby agreed, "The Caw Indians is tollerably theaveish."

The Indians had no reservations about stealing; they believed a certain amount of thievery justifiable. It represented a way of collecting toll for the use of their land. Some of the Missourians had difficulty accepting that point of view, however, since nineteenth-century white frontiersmen were not especially tolerant of Indians' rights.

Mostly though, these natives, like the majority the emigrants would meet along the way, were simply curious and anxious to trade with the travelers. Trinkets such as bells, mirrors, and beads went over big with them according to Reading but they also craved tobacco. In exchange they offered moccasins and dressed skins. Incidentally, the emigrants did not fear this tribe as they were what later generations would call "reservation Indians."

On June 1, with the long crossing finally completed, the Company set about creating their formal organization. The proceedings suggest that the labor spent in getting their wagons and stock across the Kansas had not been at the expense of their sense of humor.

Each candidate for office moved out in front of the Company with his back to the voters. Those supporting a given man then lined up behind him. At a given signal, the office-seekers began moving out across the prairie followed by their backers. As the lines grew longer, the head men began to cavort with glee, weaving and running with tail in tow, until finally the judges declared the man with the longest tail the winner. Sir William Stewart's entourage happened to be passing the emigrant encampment on election day and a newspaperman in their midst wrote about what he saw:

Here was a congregation of rough, bold, and adventurous men, gathered from distant and opposite points of the Union, just forming an acquaintance with each other, to last, in all probability, through good or ill fortune, through the rest of their days. Few of them expected, or thought, of ever returning to the states again. They had with them their wives and children, and aged, depending relatives. They were going with stout and determined hearts to traverse a wild and desolate region, and take possession of a far corner of their country destined to prove a new and strong arm of a mighty nation. These men were running about the prairie, in long strings; the leaders, — in sport and for the purpose of puzzling the judges, doubling and winding in the drollest fashion; so that, the all-important business of forming a government seemed very much like the merry schoolboy game of 'snapping the whip'. . . . 'Running for office' is certainly performed in more literal fashion on the prairie than we see the same sort of business performed in town.

The "glib-tongued orator," Peter Burnett, won election as Captain of the Company, and James Nesmith, became Orderly Sergeant. The new officers immediately created a problem for themselves by altering one of the rules of the agreement everyone had supported back in Independence.

Reading's diary entry on this date, June 1, noted that the newly elected Captain and his committeemen threw out the rule that limited each emigrant to no more than three head of loose cattle for each male over the age of sixteen in his party. Reading continued, "This subject creates much discord and entirely destroys the harmony that would otherwise prevail." He flatly predicted, "A division must take place."

Another emigrant writer, M. M. McCarver, explained, "The number of cattle is quite too large. It is impossible to guard them at night, and the Indians at this place have already commenced stealing horses and killing cattle." He, too, saw this as divisive issue, "it will be the means of a split yet, as there are a number without cattle who refuse to assist in guarding them."

The have-not emigrants were not only balking at the idea of standing guard over cattle that did not belong to them, they also complained that the large herd was slowing them down. Some of the more prosperous emigrants, such as Jesse Applegate, had brought large herds of cattle with them. (McCarver said Applegate had more than 200 head and others more than 100.)

Burnett knew this problem of loose cattle had caused some concern in the Company. He and the other leaders felt they had defused the situation, however, when they got the cattle owners to agree to make their herd available for food or replacement stock whenever necessary at a price fixed by committee. Yet, even with the compromise, it was not a happy Company that moved on towards the Blue River.

Under the newly-elected leaders, the Company divided into four marching divisions with a sub-captain in charge of each. They also began conforming to the time-honored ritual of arranging their divisions of wagons into a hollow square or circle each night for protection. This practice, developed out of the experience of the Sante Fe traders, is another example of how movies and television have distorted the common perception of the overland experience.

How many times have movie westerns shown Indians riding madly around an encircled set of wagons? A few years ago, a prominent historian conducted an extensive study of covered-wagon records to see how often that had actually happened. He could not find a single case! The Indians were not stupid. They would have been sitting ducks exposing themselves to the rifle fire from such a fortress. That is the reason emigrants always circled the wagons, it did make them safe from attack.

We should here qualify the statement that the emigrants always circled the wagons. There were occasionally some stubborn cusses who preferred to follow their own way. John Shively told the following tale about the '43 train:

> *[We] had a civil law that all the wagons should be corralled when in camp; that is, all joined in a circle. So we come to a creek which we must cross the next morning and two wagons camped nearby by themselves. Next morning while the authorities were discussing penalties, the two rebels yoked their teams and drove down to the stream to cross without orders from the Commander. The man in authority issued an order to go and stop them, and if they did not obey to shoot them. Two men were deputed to execute this decree. [When they arrived at the wagons], the foremost ox proprietor reached to his wagon bows, took down his rifle, put on a fresh cap saying, "Now you will see whether we cross or not." "In this state of affairs," says one of the detailed soldiers to the other, "George, I reckon we had better let them cross." And cross they did. And the Persian law came to naught and no powder burnt.*

Another image Hollywood loves is that of the happy emigrants milling around inside the circle of wagons. That, too, is false. The enclosure formed by the wagons served as a corral. The people camped outside. Teamsters turned their animals loose to forage for food and water when the train first stopped, but, as night came on they were driven into the encirclement. The loose cattle, meanwhile, remained outside the circle under guard. That was the crux of the division within the '43 company; such a large herd of cattle made guard duty a difficult proposition.

While on the subject of Hollywood images, it would be well to consider the picture of the family sitting up on the wagon seat behind the team. As noted earlier, most of the emigrants used oxen to propel their wagon and oxen required no harness. Instead, the driver guided his team by walking beside them and yelling out commands (sometimes using a whip or prod as reinforcement). Only those using mules for draft animals had to ride on the seat and use reins. But, since the wagons had no springs and the terrain was almost always rough, no one wanted to ride up there any longer than necessary. Often the husbands and wives would trade off for relief if they had no older son or daughter to drive for them.

Finally, those who had to anguish over a piece of furniture left behind because of fear of over-loading, would have been foolish to over-load by adding their own weight. The truth is, almost everyone walked. But oddly enough, they did not consider it a burden, especially not the women.

These people were accustomed to living on isolated farms or in small crossroads villages where women found few opportunities for socializing. Out on the prairie, however, they could spend days on end walking with friends, chatting, and picking flowers. Many of them would treasure the memory of that experience for the rest of their lives.

One way to think of an emigrant train is to imagine it as a moving community. Anything that might have gone on in a small town back in the states was likely to occur there as well. There would be births, deaths, courtship, and marriage. Some folks got along well with their neighbors, others did not. There were those who worked hard and always appeared when needed, and there were shirkers.

The biggest difference between the train and home was the close confinement and lack of privacy; little wonder that tempers sometimes flared. Fortunately, the wiser among them soon learned as Burnett did, "there was no remedy but patient endurance." He noted that at the beginning of the journey there were many "fisticuff fights" in camp but the emigrants quickly abandoned that habit and, "confined themselves to abuse in words only. The man with a black eye and battered face could not well hunt up his cattle or drive his team."

Nothing could do more injustice to these people than to glorify them or brand them as saints. They were human beings engaged in a difficult experiment that often tested them to the limit. The record shows that some simply withstood the test better than others.

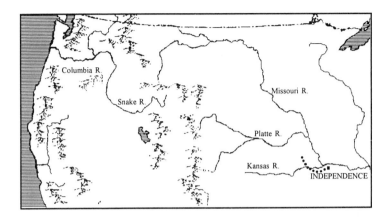

CHAPTER FIVE

Stormy Weather

Week Three: June 4 - June 10

T heir third week on the trail was one the members of the Oregon Emigrating Company would always remember. They had just finished crossing the West Fork of the Blue River in today's north-eastern Kansas when a terrific storm struck. It began the worst siege of weather they would have the entire trip.

There is nothing like a thunderstorm on the prairie. Not only does it drop rain in torrents but since there is little in the way of obstruction to absorb sound waves, the fury of noise is intensified. Overton Johnson called the rolling, crashing thunder-claps "a constant roar," and remarked that some of the sharper peals "resembled the discharge of volleys of artillery."

And then there was the lightning. Johnson described it as

41

"dazzling and incessant." For already skittish livestock, all it took
to set them to panic was a close strike. Over the years many
emigrants passing through this same area suffered the misfortune
of seeing their wagon and everything they owned careen wildly
across the land at the mercy of a frightened, stampeding team.
They counted themselves lucky if no member of their family was
in the wagon at the time.

The '43 train appears to have been more fortunate than many
of their successors, they reported no runaways and only one horse
killed by lightning. Still, it must have been a frightening experience for families with young children. Twenty-three year old
William Newby called it, "the worst storme and raine I ever saw
which commenst a bout 10 o'clock & held till day. All the tents
blode down & some holding thare waggeons to keep them from
upsetting."

Pierson Reading, too, recorded the blown-down tents and said
it put "the occupants, women and children, in a most pitiful
condition." But he also had a personal fear. He confided:

The whole atmosphere seemed charged with the electric fluid,
and during some five hours seemed a continuous blaze. I felt
much uneasiness, sleeping in the back part of a tent, at the
foot of which were six guns with the horns full of powder
near them.

The torrential downpour flooded the Blue and its tributaries
until they had overflown their banks for nearly a quarter of a mile
on either side. Water stood eight inches deep in the emigrant
camp. Sara Jane Hill, only twenty-one at the time, still remembered that night in her old age, "it even floated the ox yokes.
Where we crossed the evening before the next morning it was
forty feet deep." She also described what it was like to spend the
night:

We had double covers on our wagon. I slept in my feather

42

bed. I had a blanket and two quilts over me and all my
clothes on. There wasn't a dry thread on me. There wasn't a
yard of clothe in my bed that was not wet and I could scoop
water out with my hands.

Far more restrained, but no less effective, are these excerpts
from the diary of nineteen year-old John Boardman: Tuesday, 6th,
"Rained hard all night; all wet" on the 7th; "Rain all night; no
sleep " and for the 8th; "laying by for high water. Rain all night;
wet as usual; little sleep."

But it was not just the bedding and clothes that were saturated,
many provisions had been soaked as well. Sarah Owens recalled,
"The next morning [after the initial storm] we found about half of
our corn was wet." Her husband advised saving what they could
by turning it into bread but few followed his lead, as a result,
"thousands of pounds of meal were left by the road side." Perhaps
Peter Burnett had this incident in mind when he later wrote, "Our
emigrants, on the first portion of the trip, were about as wasteful
of their provisions as if they had been at home."

The rain-soaked ground soon became a quagmire, turning
wagon movement into an adventure. Edward Lenox described it as
"Rain, rain, rain, and mud up to the hubs of the wagons, stalled
teams, and maddened, worn out drivers." Years later John
Stoughton remembered being there as a young boy and "seeing as
many men as could get hold of a wagon working at the wheels to
get it out of the mud, the oxen having to flounder out as best they
could. I have seen them up to their sides in mire." After a couple
days of such labor it is easy to imagine that many heavy items
carelessly selected as indispensable when leaving Independence
found a new home on the muddy prairie.

By June 8th, the "maddened, worn out drivers" apparently had
expressed their wrath once too often to suit their captain for on
that date Peter Burnett resigned. He later wrote that he did so "in
consequence of ill health." He was sick all right, sick of the
responsibility, sick of the complaints. Years later he remembered,

"I adopted rules and endeavored to enforce them, but found much practical difficulty and opposition." In addition, as captain he had to select the Company's campsite each evening; so, on the 7th, he chose a spot "we supposed to be dry; but in the night another severe storm of rain succeeded, and again flooded half the encampment." The next day he quit.

Jesse Applegate, though he was one of those to succeed Burnett, understood the problem. As he saw his fellow emigrants:

They were probably brave enough but would never submit to discipline as soldiers. If the President himself had started across the plains to command a company, the first time he should choose a bad camp or in any way offend them, they would turn him out and elect some one among themselves who would suit them better.

An additional irritant creating an impasse, besides bad camp selection, was the cattle issue. Those who did not own large herds of loose stock stubbornly refused to proceed any further with those who did. The Company found itself hopelessly divided. They had little choice but to split in two. Those with more than ten head of loose stock went one way, those with less went the other.

William Martin succeeded Burnett as head of the portion of the Company without loose cattle (assuming the loftier sounding title of Colonel) and, to assist Martin, the reduced company appointed four captains, along with four orderly sergeants, to take over responsibility for each of the marching divisions.

Those with excessive cattle, comprising about sixty wagons, set up their own organization and named Jesse Applegate as leader. Under his command, the "Cow Column" as this section came to be known, divided into fifteen platoons of four wagons each. Further, Applegate ordered:

. . . each platoon is entitled to lead in its turn. The leading platoon today will be the rear one tomorrow, and will bring

up the rear unless some teamster, through indolence or negligence, has lost his place in line, and is condemned to that uncomfortable post.

From that date on the cow column acted as a completely separate train. They operated so efficiently under Applegate, however, that even with a couple thousand head of livestock to care for they had no difficulty keeping up with the others, often camping within shouting distance of their previous companions.

Jesse Applegate won lasting fame among historians by writing a splendid narrative about life in the cow column. In it he allows us to experience the beginning of a typical day:

It is four o'clock A.M.; the sentinels on duty have discharged their rifles — the signal that the hours of sleep are over — and every wagon and tent is pouring forth its night tenants, and slow-kindling smokes begin largely to rise and float away in the morning air. Sixty men start from the corral, spreading as they make through the vast herd of cattle and horses that make a semicircle around the encampment, the most distant perhaps two miles away.

The herders pass to the extreme verge and carefully examine for trails beyond, to see that none of the animals have strayed or been stolen during the night. . . . by 5 o'clock the herders begin to contract the great, moving circle, and the well-trained animals move slowly towards camp, clipping here and there a thistle or a tempting bunch of grass on the way. In about an hour . . . the teamsters are busy selecting their teams . . . to be yoked.

From 6 to 7 o'clock is a busy time; breakfast is to be eaten, the tents struck, the wagons loaded and the teams yoked and brought up in readiness to be attached to their respective wagons. All know when, at 7 o'clock, the signal to march sounds, that those not ready must fall into the dusty rear for the day. . . .

BLAZING A WAGON TRAIL TO OREGON

It is on the stroke of seven; the rush to and fro, the cracking of whips, the loud command to oxen, and what seems to be the inextricable confusion of the last ten minutes has ceased. Fortunately every one has been found and every teamster is at his post. The clear notes of a trumpet sound in the front; the pilot and his guards mount their horses; the leading divisions of the wagons move out of the encampment, and take up the line of march; the rest fall into their places with the precision of clock work, until the spot so lately full of life sinks back into that solitude that seems to reign over the broad plain and rushing river as the caravan draws its lazy length towards the distant El Dorado.

The fragmentation of the Oregon Emigrating Company taught everyone an important lesson: smaller units functioned better anyway. There had to be enough men to afford protection and provide labor for road-building and river-crossing but not so many that they would have to compete with each other for camp sites or position in the moving train. Never again would any knowledgeable emigrant company take off across the prairie with such a long string of wagons.

The smaller units did not reduce all the friction, of course; there would always be a few ruffled feathers in groups as rugged and individualistic as the Oregon pioneers. The reduced numbers were easier to manage, however, and did provide a few more interludes of harmony.

On Saturday, June 10th, the emigrants received a shock when they stumbled upon the mutilated body of an Indian. Apparently the dead man had fallen victim to a war-party of some eighty or ninety Osage and Kanzas warriors the Company had met earlier in the week. At that time those Indians had bragged of an encounter with a party of Pawnees and disgusted everyone by flourishing vestiges of human anatomy they had garnered as trophies. It now looked as though they must have collected most, if not all of them, from this one poor Pawnee.

Peter Burnett wrote back to the states shortly afterward that the Kanzas and Osages were, "the most miserable, cowardly, and dirty Indians we saw east of the Rocky Mountains." He then went on, "they annoyed us greatly by their continual begging." The Company had given the war-party some bread and a calf as they claimed to have been without food for three days; Captain Gantt had strongly advised this action to avoid having animals stolen.

Applegate's company, too, had run into this band but proved less generous than the main body. Sara Jane Hill remembered:

We had a coward in our company by the name of McArver, he wanted to make a treaty with the Indians and give them a beef but the company would not so they gave them some shirts and tobacco and moved on.

The sight of the mutilated brave and the earlier confrontation with the war-party alerted the emigrants that they were leaving the land of civilized tribes and were entering into wilder country. They would have to be more vigilant in the future and it would be a lot spookier to stand guard at night.

In that vein, Edward Lenox recalled the story of a young man, Nathan Sutton, who preceded him in guard duty one evening:

He went on guard . . . at eight o'clock, and I was rolled in my blankets, expecting to be called at twelve. At ten the crack of Sutton's gun rang out, loud and clear. In came Nate, panting and scared. "What is up, Nate?" says Captain Smith. "Oh, I shot an Indian." By this time my father was on the scene and asked, "What's up, Captain Smith?" "Nate Sutton says he shot an Indian," was the reply. At this [father] ordered the guard doubled until morning, so the Captain of the guard called us up, and stationed us thirty paces apart. You can guess there was very little sleeping that night. Daylight came. Captain Smith appeared from the guard tent, rubbing his eyes and saying, "Now, Nate, show me your

47

Indian." "Come right this way," answered Nate. "Be careful,
he may be wounded and shoot you; right here in this tall
grass, I saw him rise up, and draw his bow and arrow, and
I let him have it." Closer investigation showed that Sutton's
Indian was a large, three-hundred-dollar, yellow, Kentucky
mule, one of the four attached to the wagon of the Martin
brothers. . . . Sutton never heard the last of that shot, but all
summer long, the boys would twit him by crying out, "Oh,
Nate, when are you going to shoot another four-legged
Indian?"

Poor Nate must have been mortified, but the threat was real
and it did not pay to become too careless. The Company's own
experience, and that of later caravans, demonstrated that though
Indians could be pests and thieves, there was not much to fear
from them as long as you maintained a position of strength. Many
of the deaths attributed to Indians in later years occurred because
of foolhardiness on the part of certain whites who ignored that
simple fact.

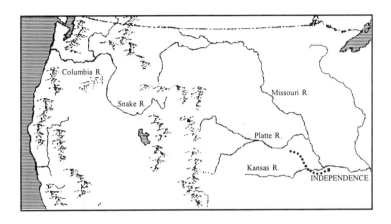

CHAPTER SIX

Indian Territory

Week Four: June 11 - June 17

I

Rain plagued the Oregon Emigrating Company for the second consecutive week as they crossed through the prairies of what today constitutes north-eastern Kansas and south-east Nebraska. They were moving north-west along the Little Blue River and had to ford several small but swollen tributaries the banks of which had turned to mire from the continual downpour. Rain is an infrequent occurrence on the Great Plains, averaging less than twenty inches per year, but most of it falls in the spring. Unfortunately for the emigrants, that coincided with the time they had to travel through the area.

49

Had it not been for the wet weather the land they covered would have been easy passage consisting as it did of rolling prairie devoid of trees except along the streams. The official designation of the area at that time was Indian Territory and it had only been part of the United States for forty years. Before that it had belonged first to the French and then to the Spanish. The United States had acquired it in 1803 as part of the Louisiana Purchase.

Louisiana originally consisted of the entire watershed of the Mississippi River. In 1682 when Robert Sieur de La Salle became the first European to descend all the way to the river's mouth, he claimed the surrounding land for France and named it for his monarch, Louis XIV. France retained possession until 1763 when, as the loser in the 4th French and Indian War, they were forced to cede the entirety of their New World holdings to Great Britain. Before that war ended, however, they signed an agreement granting all of Louisiana west of the Mississippi to Spain. Later, when the American colonies won their freedom from Great Britain in the Revolutionary War, the portion of Louisiana that had belonged to the British, i.e., everything east of the Mississippi, then became part of the new United States.

The Appalachian mountain system defined the eastern border of Louisiana. This complex system that extended from the Gaspé peninsula in Quebec, Canada to Georgia in the United States had provided a formidable barrier to expansion for Americans for more than 150 years. The peaks were not all that high, only about 4000-6000 feet, but they were heavily forested and extremely inter-folded to the breadth of about 300 miles.

The system contained several extensive ranges such as the Blue Ridge, Cumberland, Alleghanies, and Great Smokies to name a few. Since it took nearly a century and a half to discover passes over and through such a maze — this was where Daniel Boone won his fame as a path-finder — returning east once settlement began in places like the Ohio Valley and what became Kentucky and Tennessee was for many years almost unthinkable.

Thus, the geography forced farmers of the section to rely upon

50

the westward flowing Ohio River and its tributaries to move their products to market. The Ohio connected with the Mississippi to provide continuous passage by flat-boat or other water craft to the port of New Orleans. From there goods were shipped back to the east coast of the United States or on to foreign markets.

Over time, the port of New Orleans became central to the western-American agricultural system. But that port belonged to Spain. The Spanish governor, then, had considerable influence in how well the system operated. He could make it easy or difficult as he saw fit. Not surprisingly, he soon became a thorn in the side of Westerners and they began clamoring for the federal government to do something about it. Nothing came of their appeals, however, until Thomas Jefferson became president in 1800. Jefferson, an agriculturist himself, and a devoted friend of the small farmer, sympathized with the Westerners and their plight. He determined to help them by purchasing New Orleans from Spain.

Dramatically, just as Jefferson set out to solve the problem, the port changed hands again. Napoleon Bonaparte, the scourge of Europe, now had possession. At that point in history Spain had squandered the great wealth they had accumulated from their primary position in the New World — given them by the discovery of the continent by Columbus — and had become a second-rate power. When Napoleon began his conquests, then, they were easy prey.

But Napoleon was not satisfied with just the control of Europe. He, like other French nationalists, resented the loss of honor that had occurred when defeat in war had forced their country out of America in 1763. From his position of power he determined the time was right to begin the re-establishment of the French Empire in the New World. He started by forcing the Spanish rulers to return what they possessed of Louisiana to him.

Jefferson's ministers knew when they arrived in Europe to negotiate for the port of New Orleans that they faced a formidable task. In fact, for a time they thought it impossible. But they got a break when disaster intervened to swing affairs their way. While

51

the diplomatic maneuvering proceeded at a tortuously slow pace, Napoleon suffered the tragic loss of two entire armies in the West Indies.

The units had left France to take formal possession of Louisiana when they received orders to detour long enough to put down a slave revolt in the islands. What was planned as a simple diversion turned into a deadly rout. Disease and heroic blacks destroyed them.

The surprising reversal caused the disheartened Emperor to sour on his grand scheme for America. He was planning a new campaign against England and could not afford any further loss in manpower. He also needed funds. So, he instructed his finance minister to insist that if the Americans wanted New Orleans they would have to purchase all of Louisiana to get it. His price was $15 million dollars. Thus, in 1803, three astonished American envoys moved swiftly to conclude the greatest real estate purchase of all time, more than doubling the size of their country for about four cents an acre.

In 1804, flush with pride, Thomas Jefferson sent Merriweather Lewis and William Clark west to find out what he had bought. This justifiably-famous expedition followed the Missouri River to its source, crossed the Rockies to the Columbia River system, and thence to the Pacific. In the journey, the leaders and their men became the first Americans ever to travel overland to the Oregon country. The reports of their mission excited the nation and opened a whole new era in the trans-Mississippi area, helping in many ways to speed the wagons west.

In 1806, as Lewis and Clark were on their way back to the United States, another mission left St. Louis to explore south-west Louisiana. The leader of this expedition was Zebulon Pike. While the Lewis/Clark journals stimulated interest in the territory they traversed, Pike's report had the opposite effect. He declared that the land he had seen between the Missouri and the Rockies was worthless for the white agriculturalist. Later, in 1819-20, a surveying mission led by Stephen Long set out to map the entire area we call the Great Plains and in the process re-covered Pike's trail. Long, too, agreed with the earlier assessment; in fact, he gave the region the label afterwards used to identify it on maps — the Great American Desert.

The legacy of the Pike/Long expeditions was that United States policy-makers began conceiving of the idea that if the land west and south of the Missouri was worthless, it might be a great place for Indians.

Civilization had finally overrun all the tribes east of the Mississippi by the 1820's, and the Indians were suffering dearly for it. Many humanitarians, as well as Indian sympathizers, had come to the conclusion that the best course of action the nation could pursue would be to remove the natives from the vice and degradation that was destroying them in the East. And there just happened to be a perfect place available to make this possible. The dispossessed natives could finally once again "live like Indians" in the wide-open spaces of the Great American Desert.

Accordingly, in 1830, the Congress passed, and President Andrew Jackson signed, the Indian Removal Bill. From that time on treaty-makers swapped land with the Indians; in exchange for their tribal grounds in the East they were given new grants in the West. Not every tribe wanted to go, of course, and some dark tragedies in white-Indian relations occurred as a result. But eventually the more powerful whites had their way and the natives were removed out of the path of civilization into an area where they could live unmolested as long "as the grass grew green and the water flowed free."

Congress sincerely meant to establish the Great Plains as a home for the Indians. They passed laws forbidding trespass in the country; they required licenses of those trapping there; and, they set up posts to police the frontier. But, like so many good intentions about Indian lands, it worked only as long as no one cared about the country. Now, only slightly more than a decade later, the first of an eventual hundreds of thousands of emigrants were getting a close look and making their own assessment of the land their nation had declared worthless.

In the early years those passing through saw little to change their mind. This was a treeless land and they had grown up believing you needed timber to build a farm. As they saw it, trees not only proved the fertility of the soil but were necessary to provide building material for cabins, outbuildings, and fences. Further, wood was essential in cooking and heating and, for most families, it was needed to fabricate furniture. Peter Burnett revealed this deep-seated prejudice when he wrote back to an eastern newspaper, "[this] Kanzas country . . . is generally fertile, but destitute of timber, except upon the streams. . . . I saw only a few places where good farms could be made for want of timber."

It would take a few years and a few thousand Burnetts before that perception would change but when it did, Indian Territory, intended to last forever, became only a faded dream.

II

While traveling along the Republican Fork of the Blue River, the emigrants had their initial encounters with wild game. The first was an old male buffalo who had wandered off from his herd. Jim Nesmith, Captain Gantt, and four others spied him on a ridge and raced off in pursuit. They closed to within 200 yards before being spotted and then had a run of about a half of a mile before Gantt was able to discharge his pistols into the fore-shoulder. Nesmith fired his rifle, striking the quarry in the back, and another hunter fired both his carbine and a pistol into the hapless beast. In all they fired seven shots to bring him down. They were elated with their efforts though Nesmith described the meat as "very poor."

They also found antelope to be of abundance in the area. Pierson Reading described this species as an animal "about the size of a deer and of a bright color with a white spot on the hips." He said he found their flesh similar to mutton. This animal was difficult to bag, however. Extremely wary and very fast, the slightest disturbance sent them flying. Lindsay Applegate's son,

Jesse, remembered an episode in which one of his father's grey-hounds thought to make sport of an antelope that had become confused and ran through their camp. In Jesse's words:

One of the dogs, Fleet by name, pursued the antelope and the chase led across a level plain. The black dog as he sped on with all his might, looked like a crane flying along the plain. We were all excited, for the dog was gaining on the antelope at every bound and would no doubt soon overtake him. The dog thought so too, for when he was within a few yards of the antelope and expected in another bound or two to seize his prey, he gave a yelp, but that yelp seems to have been a fatal mistake, for that antelope, in a few seconds after that bark, was fifty yards away from the dog and flying over the plain as if he had been shot out of a gun. He actually passed over many yards before we could see the dust rise behind him. The dog was so astounded that he stopped short, and after gazing at the antelope for a moment, no doubt amazed beyond expression, turned about and trotted back to the train. It was said that dog would never chase an antelope afterwards.

While remarking about the game in the area, Overton Johnson declared that they found no wild fowl or smaller game until they passed the Mountains. He also noted the absence of bees after they left the Kansas River, "and this, from all we could learn, is the farthest point West which they have yet reached."

The Company now traversed Pawnee country and on the 17th of June they had an opportunity to meet with a small party of this tribe. In contrast to their earlier negative reaction to the Kanzas and Osages, the emigrants found much to admire in this particular group of natives (though Overton Johnson called them, "the most notorious rascals any where East of the Rocky Mountains"). Pierson Reading noted "they bear the character of being a proud and honorable nation." He also found them to be "best featured

Indians I have yet seen," and of some importance to him, "they are different from other Indians in one respect, they do not beg."

After reaching Oregon, Peter Burnett sent a letter back to the states containing an observation about the Pawnee that said a lot about white attitudes of that time with regard to the red man. He wrote: "They had not their heads shaved like the Kanzas Indians; but their hair was cut like white men, and they were fine looking fellows." Fine looking, since their hair was cut like ours! That mode of thinking colored Indian-white relations from the discovery of the continent.

Many nineteenth century Americans believed the only way the red man could be tolerated was to make a white man out of him. On the reservations and at the missions the natives learned to farm, to dress in "civilized clothing," and to read and write and speak in "civilized" English. In addition, missionaries endlessly debated ways of dealing with their charges. Should you turn the Indian into a Christian and then civilize him by teaching him to farm, or would it be better to civilize him first by teaching him the white man's ways and then turn him into an obedient Christian? Interestingly, nowhere in the process was there provision for the Indian to remain as he was; not even in Indian Territory.

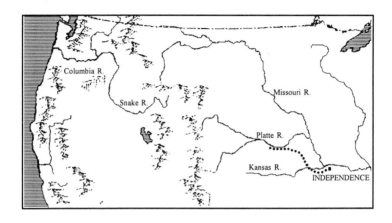

CHAPTER SEVEN

The Platte River Road

Week Five: June 18 - June 24

On the 18th of June, as their fifth week on the trail began, the Oregon Emigrating Company left the Little Blue River and crossed over a "beautiful prairie country" to the banks of the Platte River in what is today central Nebraska. This crossing of nearly thirty miles proved to be the longest they would have to endure without water in the entire route west.

Remaining close to water was crucial to a wagon train. Humans could store up a supply in casks or barrels to get them through a prolonged dry spell, but they could not carry enough for the teams and loose cattle. One full day without water, as this crossing entailed, was really pushing it. This fact alone underscored the importance of an experienced guide who knew the location of the

57

nearest water-hole or stream.

The Platte River, which flows the entire breadth of Nebraska before reaching the Missouri, was quite shallow much of the time, making it the source of a lot of droll remarks by emigrants over the years. Some described it as, "a mile wide and a foot deep," while to others it appeared, "too thick to drink and too thin to plow." Trappers had long before given up trying to use it for the transport of their furs back to St. Louis. There were so many sandbars and shallow spots that a loaded canoe spent more time running aground than it did floating.

Peter Burnett likened the Platte to the Nile, running hundreds of miles through a sandy desert. He wrote, "the course of this stream is more uniform than any I have ever seen. It scarcely ever makes a bend." The '43 train struck the river near the head of Grand Island, which they estimated to be seventy-five miles long. Timber covered the island in the middle of the stream but along the south bank, where they were, "there was not a solitary tree."

Pierson Reading described the river as:

> . . . *very shallow with a rapid current. The bottoms are from three to five miles wide, soil sandy and in many places impregnated with sulphate of soda. A ridge of high and barren sand hills [run] parallel with the river on the south side.*

He seconded Burnett with the observation, "you may travel hundreds of miles on its banks without seeing one tree."

The sterile landscape, placid river, and languid days of early summer combined to provide the following scene described by Burnett:

> *In making our monotonous journey up the smooth valley of the Platte, through the warm, genial sunshine of summer, the feeling of drowsiness was so great that it was extremely difficult to keep awake during the day. Instances occurred where drivers went to sleep on the road, sitting in front of*

Nooning on the Platte

their wagons; and the oxen, being about as sleepy, would stop until the drivers were aroused from their slumber.

Jesse Applegate remembered those dreamy Platte River days in somewhat the same way:

. . . teamsters drop asleep in their perches and even when walking by their teams, and the words of command are now addressed to the slowly creeping oxen in the soft tenor of women or the piping treble of children, while the snores of the teamsters make a droning accompaniment.

The warm, lazy days provided a welcome relief from the toil and sleepless nights of the previous two weeks, but nothing came easy for long on a wagon-train migration. Sure enough, the emigrants soon paid for their leisure by experiencing a new problem — a scarcity of fuel. They attempted to solve the shortage by collecting driftwood as they traveled, and occasionally they ran across bunches of dry willows the local Indians had used to build wigwams and then abandoned. But mostly they had to rely upon a product that, since they were now in buffalo country, came in an abundant supply. The French trappers called it *bois de vache*, but the Missourians described it less eloquently as buffalo dung or chips.

Young people on the train found themselves assigned to collecting the chips each evening. Lindsay Applegate's son, Jesse, recalled an incident that occurred to him while fulfilling that role as a seven-year-old:

> *Several of us boys were out from camp some little distance, picking them up and throwing them into piles. Our party had a pile and other parties had their piles, and as we were not far apart, it seems that we had claimed certain small districts adjacent to our respective stacks of chips, and we had to guard against trespassers. We were working hard and had become considerably excited, when, I remember, a boy about my size with yellow sun-burnt hair and freckled face (at that time I thought he had scales or scabs on his face), came over to our district and attempted to get away with a large chip, but I caught him in the act and threw another into his face with such violence as to knock off a scale and make the blood come. I think I was urged to this by the elder boys, for I remember they laughed, when I could see nothing to laugh about.*

The chips proved to be a good substitute for wood. They burned odorless and without flames, somewhat like charcoal, and generated plenty of heat for cooking. Still, it took some initial persuasion to convince many of the wives that they could use such a fuel for cooking.

Speaking of cooking, the frequent winds along the Platte forced the emigrants to devise a different arrangement than they had been using. (Perhaps the use of buffalo chips had something to do with it as well.) As Peter Burnett described, "it is necessary to dig a narrow ditch, about eight inches wide, one foot deep, and two or three feet long. This confines the heat and prevents the wind from scattering the fire."

The wind also served to make Jesse Applegate the butt of one of Sara Jane Hill's memories of the Platte River experience:

One evening we camped very late. By the time supper was ready it was dark. A few days before this the top of the lantern got mashed off, it was an old fashioned tin lantern. We lit it several times and it went out, as the wind was blowing. Captain Applegate took off his hat and placed it on top of the lantern, by the time we were done eating it had burnt a hole through the crown that you could run your fist through. One of the young men that helped drive the cattle said, 'Well, well! if the captain is that green what can you expect of the rest of us?'

An additional vexation occurred along the Platte because of the numerous buffalo that were native to the area. In the spring, during the rainy season, the buffalo would collect on the higher plains and drink from water-holes but as summer wore on and the holes dried up they would migrate towards the river and the plains near it. Curiously, in going down to the river to drink they traveled single file creating narrow paths of some six to eight inches in depth through the soft, sandy bottoms. The paths, after several years of usage, became permanently imbedded in the soil. The wagons, then, had to cross over these parallel ruts every thirty yards or so for more than one hundred miles which must have been like traveling over a giant wash-board. Talk about speed-bumps, even at two miles an hour who would want to ride then?

The jostling had one advantage though, it made it easier to make butter. Many of the emigrants had milk cows along with them and the ladies in the party soon learned that if you set a churn full of cream on the tail-gate of the wagon you could use the rough road as a labor saver in turning rich milk into butter. This well-ridged road must have served admirably.

The Platte country also provided the '43 train with an opportunity for a change in diet when Colonel Martin commissioned twenty men to secure fresh provisions for the Company. After a four-day hunt, a portion of the hunters met the train with a supply of fresh buffalo-meat. And what meat it was! As Peter Burnett would later remember, "on a trip like that, in that dry climate, our appetites were excellent; but, even making every reasonable allowance, I still think buffalo the sweetest meat in the world."

Three of the 1843 diarists happened to be assigned to the hunting party and each confessed to having less than a good time. They had the misfortune of getting caught out in the open when another prairie storm came visiting. Overton Johnson described what it was like:

> . . . *[the rain] poured down upon us as if all the windows of Heaven had been at once unbarred. The lightning and the thunder were dimming to the eye and deafening to the ear; and, withal, it was certainly just as cold as it could be without the water congealing. "I never saw it rain before," said a poor fellow, whose teeth were chattering together in a manner that seemed to threaten the destruction of his masticators. "Nor I," — "nor I," — "nor I," — echoed half a dozen others, who were as far as wet and cold were concerned, about in the same condition that they would have been had they been soaked an age in the Atlantic Ocean, and just hung out on the North Cape to dry.*

Johnson continued, since everything was wet, they could not start a fire so, "Wet, cold, and hungry we spread our beds, which were of course as wet as water could make them, and turned in; but not to sleep — it was only to dodge the wind, and shiver the night away."

Jim Nesmith, in recording the same experience said simply,

"suffered very much from a very hard, cold rain. Waded a slough and camped on a river bank among some willows. Lay in wet blankets on the wet sand. Extremely cold."

Pierson Reading became typically philosophic about the hardship. He wrote:

An uncomfortable night without fire, dinner or supper. It is to me rather hard, but there is no remedy. Misery loves company. There are twenty of us in the same situation. It is provoking to have plenty of meat in camp and suffer hunger.

Just before the storm, Reading mentioned another discomfort that vexed the emigrants. Mosquitoes. It was summer, after all, and they were traveling along the water. It seems like a small thing when read in a diary but it is easy to imagine what it must have been like. Reading observed that the animals suffered even more than the humans as they had no clothing for protection.

In many ways it was small problems such as this that made the journey across the wilderness so difficult. Especially since there was no option but to bear up; there was not the slightest chance for relief.

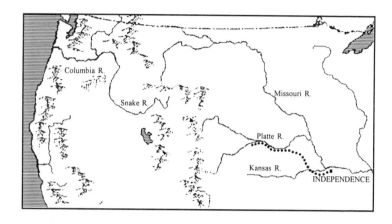

CHAPTER EIGHT

The South Platte Crossing

Week Six: June 25 - July 1

I

A s the Great Migration of 1843 traveled along the Platte River road, they were, whether they realized it or not, following a trail that western migrants had been using for at least two decades.

For several years after 1806, fur trappers slavishly followed Lewis & Clark's Missouri River route to harvest the rich crop of Rocky Mountain beaver that the expeditionary force had discovered on their way to the Pacific. Eventually, however, familiarity with the territory led to the discovery that the trapping grounds could be reached by a shorter route. Instead of staying with the Missouri River all the way to its headwaters, trappers began following the Platte and Sweetwater Rivers to the same general area. After 1825 fur-trading companies were using the new route annually in moving trade goods, supplies, and furs to and from their summer rendezvous with the Rocky Mountain trappers.

During the 1830's, missionaries and various adventurers began the practice of traveling with the fur-trade caravans each summer for protection and to guide them to their own goals in the Far West. And eventually, when emigrations to Oregon and California began, the wagon trains used the same route. Never, however, had the road been witness to anything like this year. For sheer numbers, both of people and wagons, the '43 train stood unique. Yet, within the next two decades, even their numbers would pale in comparison to the nearly 300,000 movers who would pass along the Platte River road in the process of forging a new nation with their wagon-wheels.

II

Two streams rising out of the Rockies in today's state of Colorado join to form the Platte River. The northernmost of the two, the North Platte, follows a circuitous route of 618 miles through the south-eastern corner of Wyoming before joining with the southernmost, or the South Platte (which flows 424 miles more directly east), about a quarter of the way across the state of Nebraska at a place called the Forks of the Platte. The merged waters then travel 310 miles to the Missouri. The trail the emigrants followed required them to cross both forks eventually, but the South Fork became the next big obstacle they encountered on the route to Oregon.

Earlier, on June 20th, when Colonel Martin left the main body with his hunting party of twenty men, he had taken on the additional task of scouting out a usable ford for the Company to use in crossing the river. While the group achieved some success in securing buffalo meat for the Company, they searched in vain for a place shallow enough to cross. The old joke about the Platte being only a foot deep certainly did not apply to the South Fork in the summer of 1843.

On the 26th of June the rest of the Company caught up with the hunting party and they all resumed traveling together. They had caught up with summer, too. Pierson Reading called the weather, "exceedingly warm and oppressive," while William Newby described it as "warme and swelterry." John Boardman chimed in with, "oh, the mosquitoes!"

Finally, on the 29th, still not having found a suitable ford, they abandoned the search. The train encamped in a cotton-wood grove some eighty-five miles above where the river had forked and began building some unusual ferry boats. Overton Johnson described the process:

> . . . *we procured in the first place, a sufficient number of green [fresh] Buffalo hides, and having sewed two of them together for each boat, we stretched them over the wagon beds as tight as we could, with the flesh side out, and then turned them up in the sun to dry; and when they became thoroughly dry, we covered them with tallow and ashes, in order to render them more impervious to water. (Peter Burnett said the hides were, "tacked on with large tacks.")*

While hunting buffalo to secure the skins, two separate incidents resulted in emigrants being injured by gun shots. James Nesmith was not surprised. Just a day earlier a sentinel's gun had gone off accidently and killed a mule. He wrote of that event:

> *This is the most serious accident which has yet occurred from carelessness in the use of firearms, though, judging by the carelessness of the men I have anticipated more serious accidents before this time, and if they do not occur, they will be avoided by great good luck, not by precaution.*

The careless use of firearms plagued a great many wagon trains

66

over the years, with often far more serious results than the '43 train experienced. The record reveals that 90% of gun-related accidents occurred before migrants reached the Rockies. The reason for the drastic drop-off after crossing the mountains is two-fold. One, they had left buffalo country by then, and two, they realized that they would not have to fight Indians all the way to Oregon. The result was that many men put their guns away for the remainder of the trip and the accidents declined.

On Saturday, July 1, with the boat-building completed, the Company began yet another of their experiments. They loaded their belongings into the skin-covered wagon bodies and ferried the improvised boats across the Platte. Six men were assigned to each boat. Some waded or swam along side the contraption while others pulled on a long rope attached to the front. The point of crossing measured about one mile.

Pierson Reading said that the men with the tow-ropes often had to swim with the ropes in their mouth until they could find footing. As a result they swallowed a lot of pretty bad water. Many became sick, including Reading. He described the symptoms as, "a chilliness succeeded by a high fever." Just another one of the occupational hazards of a trip across the plains.

While the skin-boats were being ferried by teams of men, further upstream where the river was not as deep but much wider, empty wagons were drawn across by teams of animals. Years later, in a newspaper interview, William Newby described that event as he remembered it:

> *The teams were all chained together in one long row. Then a long rope was fastened to the foremost team, and thirty or forty men placed on the opposite shore to pull upon the rope and thus urge and help the whole line across. It was a dangerous experiment. The water came up to the wagon beds, and the whole party landed and came out two and a quarter miles below the starting point.*

Sarah Owens, aged twenty-three at the time, later told her daughter:

> *. . . wagon beds were raised and blocked up about six or eight inches, and from forty to fifty wagons and teams were fastened together with long chains. Horses were attached to the front wagons and oxen in the rear. Then men went ahead on horseback with ropes tied to the front team. Upon reaching the other shore the men would pull in the ropes, in this way keeping the front team on the right course, while each man sat in his wagon and directed his own team.*

An elderly John Stoughton also recalled the episode, though with a slightly different slant (he had been thirteen at the time):

> *In fording the streams we sometimes had twenty wagons fastened together. I remember in crossing the Platte River our end wagons worked downstream, until they reached deep water and then rolled over and over, costing us much loss and trouble.*

That could be what Samuel Penter, then aged 28 or 29, was referring to in his later recollections when he stated:

> *. . . we tied all the wagons together. Someone had a long rope which was tied to the ring of the first wagon and men on the other side helped the train to cross. We made a good crossing except that McHaley's wagon broke loose and washed off.*

As these quotes reveal, people on the train did not always remember the various incidents in exactly the same way but, in general, when several of them make a point of discussing a particular episode years later, you may be sure it was something more than routine. Obviously this proved to be a difficult crossing even though completed, as Overton Johnson recorded, "without any serious accident."

Because the crossing of the South Platte took six days, several straggling groups caught up with the Oregon Emigrating Company including the Cow Column and another train that had left Independence the first week of June. Led by Captain J. B. Chiles, this latter group of emigrants, however, did not intend to go to Oregon. Their destination was California.

Chiles served the train as captain and guide. He qualified to function in both capacities because of his experience as a member of the first wagon train of avowed emigrants ever to leave Missouri for the Pacific coast without the protection of a fur-trader caravan. That train, too, had headed for California.

Chiles' first adventure began early in 1841 when a group of between sixty and seventy people gathered outside Independence (the figures vary depending on who you read), enticed there by some hard-sell on the part of the friends of a Missourian named John Marsh. Marsh had gone to California in 1836 along the southern route, by way of the Sante Fe trail, and wrote back telling what a paradise he had found. His friends made sure his letters received wide distribution and during the fall and winter of 1840 formed a Western Emigration Company with the specific intent of leaving for the promised land in May of 1841.

When the organizers arrived at the agreed-upon rendezvous point, however, they found only a few dozen stragglers instead of the more than five-hundred emigrants they had expected. Regardless, they were determined to go anyway. They had only one problem. They did not know how to get to California from there.

Fortunately for them, while they were mulling over how to proceed, a group of Catholic missionaries arrived who were heading west to establish a mission among the Flathead Indians. These clear-thinking men had enlisted a mountain-man to lead them. Once the priests realized how ignorant the emigrants were of what they were getting themselves in for they agreed to merge

69

with them if they would share the expense of the guide.

Once agreement had been achieved, they all left Missouri in one train consisting of fourteen emigrant wagons plus four carts and one wagon belonging to the missionaries. It was not the typical family-oriented wagon-train since it was predominantly a male group. There were, however, five women and ten children in the party. It is unlikely that many of them realized they were making history as the first wagon-train ever to head for the Pacific coast.

Everything went reasonably well, considering their small numbers, until they were near Fort Hall in today's Idaho. At that point, like Captain Gantt of the '43 train, their guide's familiarity with the route ended. The situation got stickier when they found that no one at the fort had ever tried to go to California from there. (The one man who did know the route, Joseph Redford Walker, who had once worked for Captain Bonneville, was nowhere in the vicinity.)

When this information got out, about half of the party, including all but one of the women, decided to take the safer course and follow a Hudson's Bay Brigade on to Oregon. Although they had to abandon their wagons and use a pack train the rest of the way, they had a much easier time of it than those who went on to California. That group had a horrible experience, just barely managing to stumble through without the loss of human life.

The point of the story is that the conservative went to Oregon. And over the years that tended to be the case. In fact, it became the source of a legend. According to the myth, a sign consisting of two arrows stood at the point where the trail to California split off. One arrow pointed due west with the words "To Oregon" painted on it and the other pointed south-west with a simple drawing of a pile of quartz.

As the story goes, the reckless chased the gold while those who could read went to Oregon.

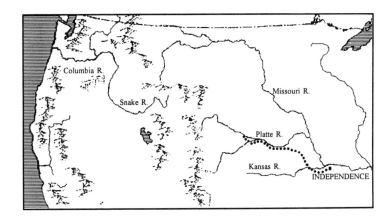

The Missionary Doctor

Week Seven: July 2 - July 8

T he Oregon Emigrating Company spent the 4th of July moving wagons across the South Platte River. Both Pierson Reading and James Nesmith made special note of the day in their respective diaries. Reading wrote, "This day is the glorious Fourth and I have spent it swimming the Platte River towing or pushing a skinboat, crossing the goods of our wagon and Mr. [Cason's]." Meanwhile, Nesmith recorded, "The glorious Fourth has once more rolled around. Myself, with most of our company, celebrated it by swimming and fording the South fork of the Big Platte, with cattle, wagons, baggage and so forth."

Each man referred to the day as the "glorious Fourth," for, indeed, that is way it was perceived in the nineteenth century. It was the biggest holiday of the year, even bigger than Christmas. Had they been back in the states almost everyone in the train would have taken part in some riotous celebration. Nesmith reflected that when he wrote:

> . . . *there seems to be some of our company ruminating upon the luxuries destroyed in different parts of the great Republic on this day. Occasionally you hear something said about mint julips, soda, ice cream, cognac, porter, ale and sherry wine, but the Oregon emigrant must forget those luxuries and, for a time, submit to hard fare.*

Reading, meanwhile, recorded disappointment, "The Oregon emigrants appear to care but very little about celebrating the glorious 4th. Not the first movement to that effect has been manifested."

Undoubtedly the hard labor had taken much of the edge off the holiday for the emigrants. With the crossing completed, however, that was a different story — at least for the young men. On their last night south of the river at the encampment they named Sleepy Grove, with all the wagons and equipment safely across, Nesmith said:

> . . . *we took, a little recreation on a sand beach, in the shape of a dance having two good violin players with their instruments. But that part of the company which is generally most interesting on such occasions, happened to be absent from our party, viz: the ladies. This deficiency was not owing to there being none with the caravan, as we have several bright-eyed girls along, but we deemed it rather unnecessary to invite them to participate in our rough exercise of kicking sand.*

During the delay at Sleepy Grove, two new members joined the Oregon Emigrating Company. The first appeared on July 1st in the person of "a fine girl infant" born to Mr. & Mrs. P. G. Stewart.

Bachelor Reading, especially touched by the arrival, noted:

This occurred in a most fortunate period while we were in camp in a most beautiful grove, with plenty of timber and delightful weather. Success to the little one, born on a journey across the Rocky Mountains.

The date of arrival of the second addition is less certain, but for most of the emigrants it carried far more significance; his name was Marcus Whitman.

He was expected. A committee of emigrants had met with him back in the Westport/Independence area prior to their departure and he had promised to join them somewhere en route. Business delayed him in Missouri until the first of June, ten days after the Oregon Emigrating Company had left. Even at that late date, however, he found stragglers just getting under way. Unencumbered with a wagon or much in the way of supplies, the doctor moved easily from train to train until he reached the main party along the Platte.

Daniel Waldo, captain of one of the straggling emigrant groups, grumbled, "I fed him the first part of the road. He had nothing to start with but a boiled ham. . . . I reckon he expected that ham to last him . . . all the way across." Even if they did have to feed him, Whitman's arrival cheered many of the emigrants. Here was a man who was not only a doctor, but also one who had been over this route twice before.

Like others in the missionary field in the Oregon Country, Dr. Whitman had been drawn there by a peculiar set of circumstances. In 1831, four Indians (three Nez Perce and one Flathead) had appeared in St. Louis with a fur-trading party returning from rendezvous. The natives were looking for what they called the "white man's book of heaven." No one knows where the Indians learned of "the book," but their appeal seemed a celestial command to the missionary societies in the East. Here were poor, benighted souls begging for help, "a Macedonian cry from the wilderness," it was called. Who could ignore that?

The first to respond were the Methodists; they chose thirty-one year old New Englander Jason Lee to carry their banner west in 1834. Lee made his way as far as the Rockies by attaching himself to a pack-train headed for rendezvous (thus establishing the pattern for later missionaries). After rendezvous, he continued farther west with a group of adventurers until reaching the regional headquarters of the Hudson's Bay Company at Fort Vancouver on the Columbia River.

The man in charge at Vancouver, Dr. John McLoughlin, welcomed Lee warmly but, in keeping with his company's policy designed to keep non-English citizens out of the area they hoped eventually would be British, he persuaded him to set up his mission south of the Columbia in the Willamette Valley; and this Lee did.

One year later a second missionary team headed west with the annual caravan in the persons of Samuel Parker and Marcus Whitman. This pair traveled west to survey the territory for the Presbyterian Missionary Board. At rendezvous they met with several Nez Perce and Flathead representatives and concluded that the field would be fruitful. Whitman headed back home with that decision while Parker went on to Fort Vancouver to scout out mission sites. (Parker later returned home by ship.)

Back in the states Whitman reported to the missionary board what he had seen and requested permission to return. The board, however, wanted only married men in the field and Marcus was a bachelor. To secure the appointment he had to find a bride. Fortunately, he had been courting a young New York woman named Narcissa Prentiss who also sought a missionary assignment. So, the two were wed.

Next, since Whitman was a doctor and not a minister, it became necessary for he and his bride to team up with a man of the cloth. The board recommended Henry Spalding and his new wife Eliza and the deal was struck. Curiously, Henry had earlier courted Narcissa himself and she had turned him down. As a result he had not formed a very high opinion of her judgement. Needless to say, it made for an interesting honeymoon trip for the Whitmans as the foursome took up the caravan route in 1836.

Incidentally, when the Whitmans and Spaldings arrived at rendezvous, they became the hit of the show. At least the wives did. It turned out that Narcissa and Eliza were the first white women ever to attend the annual mountain debauch. The Wild West was changing fast.

Once in Oregon country, Marcus and Henry set up two distinct missions; one in Cayuse country near today's Walla Walla, Washington, manned by Whitman, and the other in Nez Perce land, at Lapwai, near today's Lewiston, Idaho, with Spalding in charge. (These missions, too, were outside the land the Hudson's Bay Company sought to protect.) Unfortunately, like the Methodist Jason Lee, they found it tough going to convert their charges to Christianity.

Teachers in the field soon learned that while the Northwest tribes willingly accepted the trappings of the new religion, they continued to practice their old ways as well. After a few frustrating years the missionary boards back East grew tired of what they considered a lack of progress and began to withdraw support. Finally, in 1842, Whitman and Spalding received orders to close their missions. Incensed at the idea, and convinced the mission boards did not fully understand the problems, Marcus Whitman undertook a dangerous winter crossing back to St. Louis and thence to the East Coast to straighten out the situation.

He proved to be a persuasive advocate. The board rescinded its recall order and sent Marcus back to his post. That is how he happened to be in Independence when the Great Migration began to form.

Out of this episode, incidentally, a myth developed that Marcus Whitman, by his actions, had saved Oregon for the United States. For some time many believed that he had not only convinced the missionary board but policy-makers in Washington, D.C., as well, not to abandon Oregon. Further, in some quarters he was given credit for forming the Great Migration itself. Later studies disproved such claims, but the aura remained. In 1953, for example, when the citizens of the state of Washington had the opportunity to choose one outstanding citizen from their past to represent them in the Hall of Statuary in the nation's capital, they chose Marcus Whitman.

Judging by the reaction of the Oregon emigrants, Marcus was a sterling character, myth or no myth. Jesse Applegate declared, "it is no disparagement to others to say that to no other individual are the emigrants of 1843 so much indebted for the successful conclusion of their journey as to Dr. Marcus Whitman." James Nesmith found, "[he] possessed a great and good heart, full of charity and courage, and utterly destitute of cant, hypocrisy, shams and effeminacy, and always terribly in earnest." John Arthur remembered, "[his] persistent activity, urging the emigrants to travel, travel, as he said nothing else would carry us through."

During his trip to the East Coast that winter of 1842-3, Whitman had boarded a ferry-boat, attracting the attention of a newspaper correspondent who wrote:

Rarely have I seen such a spectacle as he presented. His dress should be preserved as a curiosity; it was quite in the style of the old pictures of Philip Quarles and Robinson Crusoe. When he came on board and threw down his traps, one said 'what a loafer!' I made up my mind at a glance that he was either a gentleman traveler, or a missionary: that he was every inch a man and no common one was clear.

How well that man judged, for it was indeed no common man who joined the Oregon Emigrating Company that summer along the Platte River road.

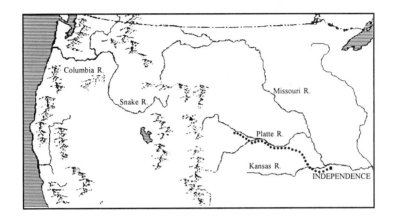

CHAPTER TEN

Sights Along the North Platte

Week Eight: July 9 - July 15

I

The five-day delay at Sleepy Grove on the South Platte River brought into focus a characteristic of the wagon-train migrations to Oregon that is often misunderstood; the wagons did not cross the plains in one long, continuous line of white-tops.

The Oregon Emigrating Company started out that way but soon split into two distinct segments because of dissatisfaction over the issue of loose cattle. During the reorganization, those divisions further split into "marching platoons." In addition, there were other segments traveling at the same time that had never been part of the Oregon Emigrating Company. For instance, there was the Califor-

77

nia company under Captain Chiles, and another group of Oregon emigrants that had left Independence at least a week later than the main body. This latter group, captained by Daniel Waldo, former Missouri neighbor and friend of Jesse Applegate, finally caught up with the main group at the South Fork of the Platte.

Overton Johnson, one of the emigration's diarists, traveled with a separate group of eight men that had split off from the main body at the Kansas River crossing. They rejoined the others from time to time, but mostly they traveled on their own.

Jim Nesmith noted, as well, that after the South Platte crossing when the Chiles and Waldo companies left the main body and moved three miles farther on before encamping, "Several wagons broke off from our company to join them, among the rest, Old Prairie Chicken. Nobody sorry." (Reading used stronger language, claiming the eighteen wagons, as he counted them, had deserted.)

So, a picture emerges of a collection of wagons in nearly a state of flux. The number in each cluster changed from week to week or day to day depending upon the mood of the drivers. Individual segments scattered for miles along the route and came together only at those places where some major obstacle forced them to bunch up. Essentially, the overall migration consisted of several trains of varying sizes traveling independent of each other.

The reality scarcely conforms to the pleasing symmetry that the images on the movie or television screen suggest. But this was real life, not art. The wagon-train experience represented pioneering at its best. No one forced people to go west, and no one could force them to conform to any situation they did not agree with as they went.

After seven weeks on the road the '43 emigrants had already encountered much hardship and disappointment and undoubtedly anticipated more. By now they understood the demands of the journey well enough to realize they could function better in smaller groups. It was only natural then to form into cliques with those they liked, trusted, and in whom they had confidence. That was a hard-nosed, independent attitude to be sure but these were hard-nosed, independent people. After all, the timid and pliable had never left home.

II

The Company, in the main, crossed over the divide between the forks of the Platte on the ninth of July and camped on the south bank of the North Platte that evening. The area they crossed was known as Ash Hollow. The terrain is cut up into many ravines and gullies and requires a steep decline to reach the shore of the North Platte. Diarists in later wagon-train companies would complain at length of the amount of effort it took to make this crossing but the 1843 migrants gave it no mention.

So far they had traveled about five hundred miles for an approximate average of ten miles per day. But Marcus Whitman was with them now and he urged them to pick up the pace. The concerned doctor rode from wagon to wagon and from group to group, constantly reminding everyone to "Travel, travel, travel; nothing else will take you to the end of your journey; nothing is wise that does not help you along; nothing is good for you that causes a moments delay." And they listened, for as Jesse Applegate said, "we knew [his advice] was based upon a knowledge of the road before us."

Along the south bank of the North Platte the emigrants entered a land of great sandstone bluffs and formations that remain some of the most famous landmarks on the Oregon Trail. Here, many of them had an experience they had never known before. They became tourists. And they were awestruck.

Most of them had lived their entire lives on isolated farms or in small cross-roads villages. They were, by late twentieth century standards, extremely ignorant of the world around them. In a time without photography or effective mass communications, nothing had prepared them for the sights the trail now offered.

Two formations in the area eventually received names that survive to this day, Court House Rock and Jail Rock. Although no

Courthouse and Jail Rocks

one in the '43 train recorded such terms in their diaries or journals, Overton Johnson was apparently looking at those curiosities when he wrote:

> *There are here several ranges of detached Sand Hills, running parallel with the River, the sides of which are almost perpendicular, destitute of vegetation, and so washed by the rains of thousands of years, as to present, at a distance, the appearances of Cities, Temples, Castles, Towers, Palaces, and every variety of great and magnificent structures.*

Next in view was Chimney Rock. Pierson Reading, Jim Nesmith, John Boardman, and several others left the encampment on the 10th of July and traveled about ten miles to get a better look at this most celebrated of all the landmarks. Reading found the formation:

> *. . . truly singular and striking. Rising from a mountain about 200 feet high and about 800 yards in circumference is a shaft or column about 15 feet in diameter and 175 feet in height.*

Chimney Rock

Both the mound or pyramid and shaft is composed of very hard sandy earth. The base is formed of a stratum of white rock.

Nesmith said, "[it] resembles a funnel reversed" and is, "one of the greatest curiosities I have ever seen in the West." Young William Newby passed the site and described it in his own inimitable way, "This mountain is a bout 250 feete high & on top thare is a bout 100 feet. Loocks like a chimney."

On the 11th of July, the emigrants could view off in the distance one of the more beautiful sights along the trail, a high range of bluffs called Scotts Bluff. This magnificent product of erosion brought out the poet in many later travelers who often used terms such as "majestic" or "sublime" in describing what they saw. The best the '43 travelers could record was Reading's observation, "These bluffs have a most romantic appearance, many of them resembling old castles." Overton Johnson dismissed them as, "a range of high Sand Hills," but was fascinated by what he called, "the melancholy circumstance" of how the bluffs received their name.

Indeed, the story of the last days of Hiram Scott for whom the

Scotts Bluff

bluffs were named has been told and retold so many times over the years by travelers through the West that the truth is totally lost. There are enough versions to fill a book. In 1843, however, a reporter with Sir William Stewart's hunting expedition recorded a version he heard in the area from one of his traveling companions, William Sublette. This may come closest to the truth since, at the time of the "melancholy circumstance," Scott was an employee of Sublette's. It goes something like this.

In 1828 Hiram Scott was one of the men in charge of the pack train bearing supplies to the rendezvous of that year on the Green River in today's Wyoming. While at the gathering he grew deathly ill and was unable to move when it was time for the train to return to St. Louis. The pack train leader assigned two men to stay behind and take care of him until he improved while promising to wait for them farther on at the bluffs along the Platte.

A few days later, when Scott felt strong enough to ride a horse, the three men moved out, but soon the ill man became so weak he could no longer stay in the saddle. So, his companions shot a couple of buffalo, built a boat with the skins and a frame of willow branches, and began transporting him by water. They made rapid progress until they struck some rapids where the boat was broken up and they barely escaped drowning. In the disaster they lost all of their supplies and belongings, guns included. They found themselves reduced to subsisting upon what they could gather or scavenge along the way.

After nine days, physically exhausted from carrying Scott, and near starvation from the lack of adequate food, they finally arrived at the bluffs of the Platte only to find the pack train had gone on without them. Panic stricken, the two guardians concluded that to stay any longer with the dying man would be to perish with him. It appeared obvious to them that he was beyond hope, so, "without daring to say farewell," they left him.

(Here I deviate from the reporter's tale to a popular version of what happened next.) After further trials, the two eventually made it back to civilization where they reported to the company that Scott had died and they had buried him on the trail. The next summer William Sublette personally led the pack train to rendez-vous and as he passed through the narrow bluffs he stumbled upon the scattered bones from what he could identify to be Scott's body. To his horror he realized that the remains were several miles from where he understood the burial had taken place. Obviously his men had told a lie. He knew then that they had abandoned their charge to his fate and that the poor man had crawled for days before he died.

Sublette never revealed the names of those who treated Hiram Scott with such callousness but the spot where the infamy took place has ever since borne the name, Scotts Bluff.

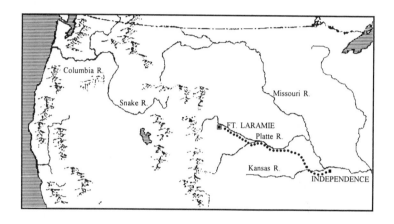

CHAPTER ELEVEN

Fort Laramie

Week Nine: July 16 - July 22

I

A day or so after leaving Scotts Bluff, the Oregon Emigrating Company crossed what would become the border separating today's states of Nebraska and Wyoming. Their route now carried them along the foothills of the Laramie Mountains into Sioux and Cheyenne country. Jim Nesmith saw many of the boys "busily engaged in scouring up their old rifles and making other arrangements preparatory for Indian fighting."

In the earliest years of the Oregon emigrations, many men believed that the Indians would resist the crossing of their lands. Accordingly, they left Missouri fully armed and mentally prepared

84

to fight their way across the plains. The '43 train had already experienced a scare or two with the Kanzas and Osage tribes. So, the thought of encountering the more notorious upper-plains Indians filled them with anxiety. Though there were some nervous moments, once again their worst fears proved groundless.

Peter Burnett recounted an incident in which one young white hot-head nearly caused a serious confrontation with a group of Cheyennes by insulting their chief:

I saw that trouble was coming, and I followed the chief, and by kind, earnest gestures made him understand at last that this young man was considered by us all as a half-witted fool, unworthy of the notice of any sensible man; and that we never paid attention to what he said, as we hardly considered him responsible for his language. The moment the chief comprehended my meaning I saw a change come over his countenance, and he went away perfectly satisfied. He was a clear-headed man; and, though unlettered, he understood human nature.

Burnett also felt the Indians left them alone because, "they saw we were mere travelers through their country and would only destroy a small amount of their game. Besides, they must have been impressed with the due sense of our power."

The tension over possible Indian problems was soon offset by the joy of arriving at a lonely outpost in the south-east corner of today's Wyoming. In a land of sparse, arid hills, where the days were hot and the nights were cold, the Oregon Emigrating Company arrived at Fort Laramie. They finally had the opportunity of relishing their first taste of civilization in eight weeks.

Laramie, a privately-owned, fur-trading post, occupied a commanding position on high ground above the Laramie River, which emptied into the Platte two miles below the Fort. Just one year earlier John Charles Frémont had visited there and in his journal left a contemporary description:

85

Fort Laramie

The walls are about fifteen feet high, surmounted with a
wooden palisade, and form a portion of ranges of houses
which entirely surround a yard of about one hundred and
thirty feet square. Every apartment has its door and window
— all of course, opening on the inside. There are two
entrances, opposite each other and midway the wall, one of
which is a large and public entrance, the other smaller and
more private — a sort of postern gate. Over the great
entrance is a square tower with loopholes, and, like the rest
of the work, built of earth. At two of the angles, and diago-
nally opposite each other, are large square bastions, so
arranged as to sweep the four faces of the walls.

The high walls provided a welcome sight to trail-weary
emigrants. Many in the Company must have shared the feelings
expressed by Narcissa Whitman in a similar situation during her
crossing of the plains in 1836. Then she had confided in her
journal, "Anything that looks like a house makes us glad."

Those emigrants interested in the history of the Fort learned that it had recently been relocated and rebuilt. The original structure, built in 1834 of cottonwood logs, had stood on a site about one mile closer to the river's mouth but after a few years it had begun to rot so badly that a new facility constructed of adobe replaced it in 1841. From the beginning the post had been intended to serve as a collection point for buffalo skins.

The original owner, William Sublette, had spent many years in the beaver trade when he began to realize that the business was dying and it was time to diversify. The shaggy buffalo skin was just then coming into its own as a trading commodity because of its increasing popularity back east as a throw rug in front of a fireplace or as a lap robe in an open sleigh. Sublette knew that most white trappers would never stoop to the hunting of such a product; it was beneath their dignity. So, he determined to build up the business by trading with the local tribes of Sioux and Cheyenne Indians.

He considered a fixed post necessary to provide protection to white traders and as a convenience for the nomadic tribes that he expected to bring in hides for exchange. Of course, free trappers were encouraged to bring in beaver pelts as well, but the primary business of the fort was with the Indians.

One of the things that helped spur construction of the new, improved Fort Laramie was a rival fur company that moved into the territory in the fall of 1840 with the audacity to build their post on the same stream only a mile away, nearer the mouth. The newcomers called their post Fort Platte and set up a lively competition for the local trade. (Interestingly, though the Oregon Emigrating Company set up camp opposite Fort Laramie, "The boys at Fort Platte" as Jim Nesmith called them, "gave us a ball in the evening, where we received hospitable treatment.")

Laramie's facilities provided the emigrants with an invaluable opportunity to do some work that could not be accomplished on the open prairie, such as blacksmithing and wheel repair. While the men used the fort's forge and carpentry shop, the women spent the layover catching up on laundry and other domestic chores. As one further service, the Fort put their boats at the disposal of the Company for use in ferrying wagons across the Laramie River.

Despite the civility and hospitality, both forts proved a disappointment to those emigrants who had hoped to replenish dwindling supplies. These were fur-trading posts, not general stores; they simply were not equipped to handle emigrant traffic. What provisions they did part with, they held dear. Peter Burnett found, "Coffee, $1.50 a pint; brown sugar, the same; flour, unbolted, 25 cents a pound; powder, $1.50 a pound; lead, 75 cents a pound; percussion caps, $1.50 a box; calico, very inferior, $1.00 a yard."

One excuse for the high prices, perhaps, was Pierson Reading's observation, "The stock of goods is at this time almost exhausted and they are daily looking for a supply brought across from the Missouri River, which is about 250 miles." Of course, the fact that there was no competition did not hurt matters either.

Somewhere along this stretch, whether at the Fort or earlier is not specified, the Company experienced its first turnarounds. A turnaround was simply that, an emigrant who decided for one reason or another to give up and go back home. Jim Nesmith talked about this phenomenon years later in a address before a convention of Oregon Pioneers:

> *Their hearts weakened at the prospect of the toil, privations and dangers of the trip and the great uncertainty of its termination. In view of all the surrounding circumstances then existing, I am of the opinion that those who turned back manifested more discretion, but less valor than those of us who braved the dangers and uncertainties of the trip.*

Psychologically, those who turned back knew they could be branded as quitters, if not cowards; so, they had to find a satisfactory explanation for their action. Over the years, many false tales of epidemics or Indian atrocities had their source in desperate attempts at justification by just this kind of person.

One family that returned to Missouri from the '43 train, for example, convinced their relatives, "After traveling for some time they were compelled to turn back on account of some Indian depredations." Yet, not one such instance was recorded by the diarists that year or remembered in later recollections. In fact, Jesse Looney wrote his brother as soon as he arrived in Oregon to report that "Upon the whole we fared better than we expected. We had no interruptions from the Indians."

Sometimes, though, people did not have to fabricate a reason for turning back. They simply no longer had the heart to go on after suffering the loss of a loved one. Just such an excuse (though they did not use it) existed for a family traveling with the Cow Column of the Oregon Emigrating Company.

On July 18th, a few days beyond Fort Laramie, while traveling over what William Newby described as a very bad road, six-year Joel Hembree, out of sheer boredom, was riding on the tongue of his father's wagon when a sudden jolt threw him off and before anyone realized what had happened, both the front and the back wheels passed over him. He managed to linger one day before becoming the first fatality on the '43 train.

Imagine how the family felt. Surely no one would have blamed them if they had decided to turn back while it was still shorter to return to Missouri than to go to Oregon. But, though their hearts must have ached, they did not quit. The diary entry of William Newby says, "We buried the youth & in graved his name on the head stone. Traveled 17 miles."

II

The Oregon Emigrating Company now traveled through an area known as the Red Buttes as they approached the spot where they planned to cross the north fork of the Platte River. Overton Johnson described the buttes as, "occupying a space of many miles in extent, and a large portion of the earth and stone, of which they are composed, is as red as blood."

On Sunday, July 22, when the Company reached the fording spot, they had, by their estimate, traveled 736 miles from Missouri. They were trail-hardened veterans by now and accomplished a difficult crossing with considerable ease, suffering only one mishap. Of course, that single mishap was of some importance to the man involved. William Newby had an experience that provided story-telling material for the remainder of his life.

In his diary the twenty-three year old recorded that the Platte was indeed shallow enough to ford but it had "a current like a mill tale." So, before he crossed he "toock the most of my thing out of my waggeon & tide it to a nother one and it turned over & over & come luce & washed down the river." He and two other men then, "follerd after it a bout one mile & had all like to got drowned. We found it a bout 3 miles down the river. We got it out with out much damage. I lost my gun & shot pouch, ax, tare bucket & oxyoake."

In an unusual reversal, during the fording of the north fork the slower Cow Column crossed first while the main company delayed with several men sick. Jim Nesmith called it a kind of fever. But it was more than just physical illness that beset the emigrants as this segment of his diary reveals:

> *The company discontented and strong symptoms of mutiny. Some anxious to travel faster, some slower, some want to cross the river here, some want to go ahead, and others want to go any way but the right way. This will always be the difficulty with heterogeneous masses of emigrants crossing these plains. While every man's will is his law, and lets him act or do as he pleases, he will always find friends to support him. In order to obviate this difficulty and maintain good order in large companies, the presence of military force, and a declaration of martial law is highly necessary. Then emigrants will travel in peace, harmony and good order. They have the elements of destruction within themselves.*

Jim obviously knew what he was talking about though his solution was a bit drastic. His testimony serves to reinforce that of Peter Burnett and Jesse Applegate: these were difficult people to lead. But the episode with the Hembree boy demonstrated that they had courage too, and in the final accounting, it was the courage and not, "the elements of destruction within themselves" that came out on top.

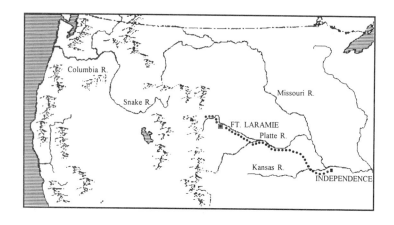

CHAPTER TWELVE

Independence Rock

Week Ten: July 23 - July 29

D uring the last week in July, the Company left the prairies for good and entered the shrub-covered basin area of central Wyoming. To the south of them lay the Laramie Mountains and directly ahead the Rockies. They traveled for two days south-west along the north fork of the Platte through an area in which, according to Overton Johnson, "we suffered considerably for the want of water — the little we found [was] strongly impregnated with a kind of salt, prevalent almost everywhere in the neighborhood of the Platte." This was a new trial for the emigrants — alkali.

There had been alkali-infested pools of water along the Platte earlier as well but with fresh water close by those pools offered no temptation to the stock. Now, though, the trail wound some distance from the main stream across a land so barren and dry that the moving wagons stirred up one continuous, billowing cloud of dust. Dust, dust, dust! Dust so saturated with alkali that it not only choked, but nearly blinded the teams.

To the suffering animals any pool was a source of relief. Since it was nearly impossible to tell for certain which pools were safe and which were not, it took considerable vigilance for the tired teamsters and drovers to keep the poor beasts from poisoning themselves. That problem would not exist for later emigrants. After a few years bleached bones and rotting carcasses easily identified the pools to avoid.

The humans suffered from the dust as well, of course. It filled every pore and made life miserable for all breathing creatures. And then there was the heat. It was late July and the temperatures soared without relief. Sunburn and dehydration added to the discomfort. Children cried, humans cursed, and the poor animals plodded along without understanding why they should be driven away from tempting water holes. People who just a few weeks earlier had complained of the incessant rain would have given anything for a downpour.

Fortunately, after two days of suffering they received a reprieve when they came upon what Johnson described as, "a beautiful spring, of very clear cold water, rising in a green valley, through which its water flows about one mile, and sink in the sand." This was Willow Springs.

They stayed one full day at the oasis and sent out hunting parties to replenish their supply of fresh meat. This time, however, they found the buffalo scattered and hard to find, a situation Overton Johnson attributed to what he called a "pleasure party" that happened to be in the vicinity.

The party that attracted Johnson's wrath had left Independence around the same time as the emigrants and had followed about the same route, but under a totally different circumstance. They were what today would be called a bunch of tourists. Their organizer and leader was a Scottish aristocrat named Sir William Stewart. He was making his sixth expedition to the land he had fallen in love with when, as a guest of William Sublette, he had attended the summer rendezvous of 1834. His party this year consisted of about sixty men, including hired hands, invited guests, and personal servants.

As Johnson saw it, Stewart's people, by staying several days ahead of the emigrant trains:

> . . . *[were] running, killing and driving the game out of our reach. It was cheap sport for them, but dear to us; and we were lead to conclude, that if ever again an English or Scottish nobleman sees fit to look for pleasure in the Rocky Mountains, while an emigrating party is passing over them, it will be prudent to place him in the rear, instead of the van.*

Stewart and his friends were not the only non-emigrants passing through the Rocky Mountain country that busy summer of 1843. From time to time the emigrant trains had occasion to camp near a United States government surveying expedition engaged in mapping the trail for the future. This expedition had at its head a man who would one day win renown as, "The Pathfinder," though the emigrants of '43 gloated that the path he found was the one they made. His name was John Charles Frémont.

Frémont had left Independence several days after the Oregon Emigrating Company, about the same time as the California Company and Daniel Waldo's straggling Oregon emigrants. The wagon-train path would cross that of this famous surveyor more than once before they reached Oregon.

The emigrants left Willow Springs on the 26th of July and the next day arrived at a tributary of the North Platte called the Sweetwater River. The Sweetwater, a pure, clear mountain stream supposedly got its name from an incident in which a fur-trapper's mule fell into the steam and lost a pack containing sugar. But it likely would have received that name anyway from the emigrants

94

who could certainly appreciate its delicious water after crossing the dry, alkali basin.

At the point where the Oregon emigrants reached the Sweet-water River there stands a large, granite, turtle-shaped mass called Independence Rock. This name, too, is a product of mountain-man lore. William Sublette dubbed it that when he and a large party of trappers spent the 4th of July there in 1830.

The members of the '43 train had the distinction of being among the earliest pioneers to paint their names upon the mono-lith. Several mountain-men, explorers, and missionaries had preceded them, but very few emigrants. In time, the rock would come to be so covered with names that it was known as the regis-ter of the desert.

Jim Nesmith had been out with a hunting party when the Oregon Emigrating Company reached Independence Rock; when he rejoined his companions he found the Company had split again. Colonel Martin with his following had gone on ahead leaving a disgruntled group behind. As Nesmith recorded it in his diary:

Our wagon and some others of his [Martin's] company fell in with some deserters from Applegate's company making in all nineteen wagons. . . . The Oregon emigrating company has been strangely divided, and no doubt the dividend will be again divided. The materials it is formed of can not be controlled.

As the week ended fragments of the Company were scattered along the Sweetwater. Nesmith's new band stayed on an extra day at the foot of the Rock to dry meat and get organized. Captain Cooper assumed command of the splinter group and young Jim now found himself stripped of the title Orderly Sergeant. As he solemnly wrote in his diary, "I mount guard as a private tonight for the first time on the trip."

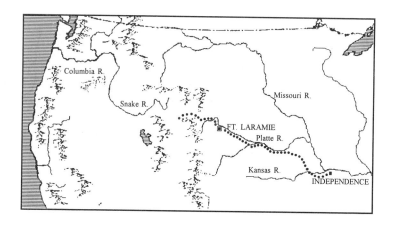

CHAPTER THIRTEEN

Death, Disease and Acts of Deity

Week Eleven: July 30 - August 5

I

On Sunday, July 30, as the Oregon Emigrating Company began its eleventh week on the trail, Jim Nesmith, with several other young men, escorted, "five or six young ladies" to Independence Rock where he, "had the satisfaction of putting the names of Miss Mary Zachary and Miss Jane Mills on the Southeast point of the rock, near the road, on a high point." He described his inscriptions as, "Facing the road, in all the splendor of gunpowder, tar and buffalo grease." This mixture of gunpowder and grease was the accepted method of recording names on the granite surface as it was too hard to carve. (John Boardman of the '43 California

96

Independence Rock

Company said the rock "appears as if cemented together with cast iron.")

Nesmith described the landmark as:

> . . . *an unshappen pile, about half a mile long, and half that breadth, and 100 feet high. The composition of the rock is a flinty, gray substance, mixed with limestone and very hard. Sweet Water River runs by the foot of it about fifty yards distant, and a great many high mountains and peaks are in the neighborhood.*

Jim's usual companion, Pierson Reading, missed the fun at Independence Rock as he was ill with a form of vertigo. In the accepted practice of the time he attempted to bleed himself to get rid of the "bad blood" but without success. Finally, after spending several days riding in the wagon, he called upon the services of Marcus Whitman. His diary shows that his illness had not been at the expense of his sense of humor; he wrote, "Have taken medicine and was bled by Dr. Whitman who cut an orifice in my arm large enough for a beaver to make his ingress."

Despite his attempts at levity, Reading suffered from a severe form of what the emigrants called, "mountain fever." The ailment received that label because it appeared only after leaving Fort Laramie and upon approaching the Rockies. Modern diagnosis suggests it might have been Rocky Mountain spotted fever or Colorado tick fever, but in any case, it was serious. Over the years it was the second most common cause of death by disease, exceeded only by cholera.

It is surprising more emigrants did not succumb to illness considering their total lack of understanding or practice of elementary hygiene. One factor that helped protect them from their ignorance was the necessity for constant movement; they rarely stayed in one camp longer than a day or two and so avoided the spread of contagion that would have been the consequences of their unhealthy habits.

No one at that time had any idea of germ theory, including medically trained men like Whitman, so tainted water became a real danger. The emigrants frequently obtained water from stagnant pools when nothing else was available and it was only by accident that they might boil it before drinking, such as when they used it to make coffee.

Sara Jane Hill recorded a typical incident. As she set the scene, her segment of the train had been a long spell without water and when they finally found some, "it was a buffalo pound. We had to take a bucket and hit the water to get the bugs away before you could dip a bucket of water, then had to strain it before making coffee."

Pierson Reading eventually recovered from his bout with the fever (and the induced bleeding), but a fellow traveler was not so fortunate. On August 4, the Company suffered its second fatality when an emigrant from Arkansas, Clayborn Payne, succumbed to what Jim Nesmith called an inflammation of the bowels. He had been one of the men earlier reported ill after leaving Fort Laramie, and, like Reading, had suffered from high fever. He left a wife and four children. Nesmith confided in his diary that he found it sad "to see a fine, stout young man reduced to a wreck by disease, far from his home and friends."

Jim made an interesting point. Death on the trail, though statistically no more frequent than would have been expected back in the states, had a special poignancy. Peter Burnett described it well, "We buried him [Payne] in the wild, shelterless plains, close to the new road we had made, and the funeral scene was most sorrowful and impressive. Mr. Garrison, a Methodist preacher, a plain, humble man, delivered a most touching and beautiful prayer at the lonely grave."

Many families like the Paynes confronted spending the remainder of their lives recalling just such final mournful scenes; they knew they could never return to the wilderness site of their loved one's "lonely grave."

The Company now camped with the snow-capped Rockies in view and Peter Burnett found it to be, "a grand and magnificent sight" as he had, "never before seen the perpetually snow-clad summit of a mountain." (He was looking at the Wind River Range.) The nights turned cold at this elevation, laying a thin layer of frost on the dew-moistened grass and freezing water in the camp kettles. William Newby said, "It is cool enough of nit[e]s for a man to set in a stove room with a over cote on."

The nightly freezing did much to neutralize unhealthy camp-ground habits, and though the emigrants did not know that, they could recognize the effects. Overton Johnson, for one, became enthusiastic about the country, exclaiming:

> . . . *the pure Mountain air and the rough wholesome manner of living have already restored many who were before feeble and afflicted to health, strength and activity; and we are convinced they are better remedies for constitutional or pulmonary diseases than all the Patent Medicines and learned prescriptions, with which the public have ever been gulled.*

99

Men such as Pierson Reading who had survived the bout with mountain fever and now felt restored to health could certainly agree.

II

The route along the Sweetwater was quite easy going though to the north it featured a high, broken, barren, and detached formation of rocks extending for miles in parallel with the road. (Frémont's maps described them as "Ridges and masses of naked Granite destitute of vegetation.") The massive formations included two more noted curiosities of the trail. The first, called Devil's Gate, stood about four miles from Independence Rock.

Devil's Gate is formed by the river flowing directly through a narrow chasm of almost perpendicular rock. Overton Johnson estimated the walls of the chasm to rise about three hundred feet above the water. Fortunately the wagon-train did not have to pass through the Gate as that would have been impossible. Instead they could admire the sight from a distance as they traveled around the mountain the river had chosen to cut through. As Theodore Talbot of Frémont's surveying party noted:

It appears strange that this stream should force its rude passage through lofty rocks, when there is a natural depression of the country, on the very same course and only a few hundred yards distant. This is a place to contemplate the wondrous ways of the Deity.

The second landmark stood off in the distance and remained in view for at least a day's travel. Called Split Rock, this granite formation with a V-shaped opening at its peak provided an unerring guide line to follow.

The week along the Sweetwater featured the company's first recorded trial by jury and one more example of fragmentation. Jim Nesmith wrote that the committee found "Old Zachary" guilty of defrauding a young man out of his provisions and stranding him in the wilderness. His punishment, according to Nesmith, was ejection from the train and, "the old rogue, with the two Oteys, is encamped about a mile ahead alone; a small camp but a big rascal."

As the week drew to a close, the emigrants experienced an unexplained phenomenon. Early on a clear, cloudless, Friday afternoon, they heard a sound Jim Nesmith described as, "a loud, sharp report, seeming to be in the air directly above us, and resembling the report of a piece of heavy artillery." John Boardman called it, "one clap of thunder that sounded like a cannon," while William Newby wrote:

Thare was a very curious explosion at noon; first thare was some thing past over us in the element like a bawl of fier, then follwd it a long streek of blew smoke in a zig zag form a bout 2 hundred yards long. Then followed it a very tremendious report as if it had bin large guns firing."

From Newby's description it sounds like a meteor, but whatever it was it is a delight to read his account.

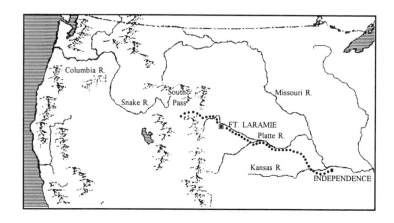

CHAPTER FOURTEEN

South Pass

Week Twelve: August 6 - August 12

I

T wo days into their twelfth week on the trail the Oregon emigrants slept on what Overton Johnson called the Backbone of North America. They had reached the continental divide at a place known as the South Pass.

This gradual saddle over the Rocky Mountains is the most significant segment of the entire road. It is the only place where wheeled vehicles could cross the Rockies; without it there might never have been an Oregon Trail.

Johnson wrote, "both the ascent and descent were so gradual, that, had we not been told, we should have passed over the

102

dividing ridge in the Rocky Mountains without knowing it." John Boardman recorded, "on the very height of the pass of the Rocky Mountains one would imagine himself on an extended plain, with mountains on either side and a level country in front of him, one does not know when he crossed the mountains." William Newby agreed with his fellow travelers, "The mane mountain is a graduel desente up & allso the same down. If you dident now it was the mountain you woldent now it from aney outher plane."

The mountain-men had long been familiar with the South Pass, having crossed it many times to and from their annual rendezvous. But the initial discovery by a white man occurred in 1812 and is part of the story of one of the great adventures that helped establish the United States's rights to the Oregon Country. It all began with the publication of the Lewis & Clark journals.

When John Jacob Astor, then the wealthiest man in the United States, read of the abundance of beaver the explorers had found in the streams of the Rocky Mountains, he struck upon a scheme to make himself even richer.

For some time he had been envious of the money made by maritime traders engaged in dealings with the natives of the north Pacific coast of America. These sea-going fur-traders swapped trinkets for sea-otter pelts and then exchanged the pelts in China, where they were highly prized, for tea, silk and spices. As Astor conceived it, he would combine the sea-otter trade with the harvest of Rocky Mountain beaver and control the entire venture from a fixed post at the mouth of the Columbia River. At the time there were no white settlements in the entire Northwest.

Astor sent out two parties to accomplish his purpose, one by land and one by sea. The sea-going segment carried tools, materials, and supplies to erect and operate a fort while the overland party intended to scout out sites for sub-posts and the means of getting started in the beaver trade on their way to rejoining the others. Unfortunately, each mission turned into a disaster.

The ship, called the *Tonquin,* reached the mouth of the

Columbia, disembarked men enough to begin construction of the post that they named Astoria in honor of their patron, and then sailed off again to engage in the sea-otter business. While trading with a group of Indians, however, a confrontation ensued that resulted in the murder of the entire crew and the destruction of the ship.

Meanwhile, the overland group became hopelessly lost en route from St. Louis while seeking a short-cut to the Rockies. The men scattered into small parties, each trying to find their own way, and endured a series of horrible trials before stumbling in, a few at a time, to the new post. They had left St. Louis in October of 1810 and the final remnants did not arrive at Astoria until February of 1812.

But their troubles were not over. In 1812 the United States went to war with Great Britain and it just so happened that several of the Astorians were Canadian citizens. Their loyalties received a severe test when a group of Canadian fur-trappers belonging to a rival fur-trading company out of Montreal showed up, intent upon establishing their own post in the area. These new arrivals notified the Astorians that a British war-ship was on its way to claim the newly-built post as a prize of war.

By this time Astor's men had grown sick of the entire affair. They arranged to sell out to the Montreal traders in exchange for safe passage back home. A group of loyalists, however, chose to return to the United States overland and report to Astor what had happened. It was this group, headed by Robert Stuart, that discovered the South Pass.

The heritage of the Astorian adventure, besides the discovery of the Pass, was that during the negotiations to settle boundaries at the end of the War of 1812, the United States could assert that its citizens had begun occupation of the Oregon country prior to the war, and before any other nation, and that such occupation had ceased only under duress. Great Britain agreed.

In 1819, therefore, a formal ceremony was held in which a group of dignitaries of both nations gathered at the site of Fort

Astoria to take down the British flag and run up the Stars and Stripes, thus declaring to the world American rights to the location.

Once the ceremony and festivities had ended and the delegates had sailed away, the Canadians replaced the American flag with their own and resumed business as usual. The entire incident seemed petty and meaningless at the time, but Americans now had the force of international law behind their claims to precedence in occupation of the Oregon country.

The Montreal traders, incidentally, had renamed the post Fort George and continued operating it until their merger with the Hudson's Bay Company in 1821. Later, in 1825, the HBC abandoned the post when they established their new headquarters at Fort Vancouver.

II

As the emigrants crossed over the South Pass they had traveled 836 miles from Missouri and were officially entering Oregon. An unimpressed Jim Nesmith was one of the few to note the fact, "We now consider ourselves in Oregon Territory, and we consider this part of it a poor sample of the El Dorado." Theodore Talbot agreed; he wrote, "Today we fairly set foot in Oregon Territory. . . . 'The land of promise' as yet only promises an increased supply of wormwood and sand."

Over the years few diarists thought about being in Oregon once they crossed the continental divide. To most emigrants Oregon meant the Willamette Valley. It is easy to understand why they felt that way in the initial two decades of emigration since no one settled east of the Cascades until 1861. Yet, that image of the Willamette Valley as Oregon has never died.

During this week the emigrants both gained and lost a member. On the 6th of August John Pennington's wife gave birth to a daughter, and on the 9th a young man named Stevenson died of the fever contracted near Fort Laramie. Once again the emigrants faced a mournful task. Pierson Reading noted that the dead man was from Kentucky and then wrote, "They deposited the remains of this poor fellow on the bank of the creek, far distant from his native home. In all probability none of his relations will ever know his resting place."

Many must have found it hard to swallow as they walked away from that grave, wondering if this trip would end like that for them. Oregon would have to be a wonderful place to make all this worthwhile.

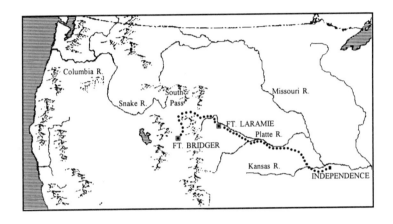

CHAPTER FIFTEEN

Fort Bridger

Week Thirteen: August 13 - August 19

I

T he middle of August found the Great Migration camped beside Pacific Spring and near the halfway point in their journey. The spring was the source of the first body of water they encountered flowing west, Pacific Creek. Here, the ladies in the Cow Column found a delightful opportunity to vary their families' diet. As Sara Jane Hill remembered:

> *. . . we found plenty of blue gooseberries maybe you think it wasn't a treat, every woman and child was out with its bucket or cup. We had some of the finest dumplings for dinner you*

ever seen in your life.

From Pacific Creek the trail crossed the various branches of Sandy Creek, a tributary of the Green River, until intersecting with the main stream itself in the south-west corner of today's Wyoming. By arriving so late in the summer, the emigrants could ford the Green without difficulty though in many emigration years, when the trains were able to get an earlier start, this crossing could be treacherous.

This wild and beautiful body of water flows south out of Wyoming through today's Flaming Gorge Reservoir into Utah. From there it curls east long enough to catch the extreme north-west corner of Colorado before returning to Utah where, in the south-east corner of the state, it joins the Colorado.

Leaving the Green behind, the train headed south towards one of its tributaries, Hams Fork, and found themselves traveling through a desert as arid as anything they had encountered earlier. John Shively told what it was like:

The glare of the sun on the desert is sickening. No water for many miles, but on looking around you see a lake or river on your right or left. It is not far to the lake. Off I go. I get no nearer the lake. It is a mirage caused by the glare of the sun through the dry atmosphere on parched earth.

The animals too, saw the lake and rivers and drove their teamsters and drovers crazy trying to keep them on the trail.

The loaded wagons and plodding stock pulverized the parched earth and once again the emigrants traveled through clouds of billowing dust. The flying dirt and intense heat forced drivers to be especially attentive to creaking hubs and loosening tires.

The hubs required constant attention, regardless, which is why every wagon had what the emigrants called a tar bucket suspended from the rear axle. (The bucket did not actually contain tar but rather a form of grease made from rendered animal fat.) The iron

Fort Bridger

tires, however, became a new problem because of the dry mountain air.

Peter Burnett wrote back to a New York newspaper after his arrival in Oregon and warned of the situation, "When you reach the mountains, if your wagon is not well made of seasoned timber, the tires become loose." He explained that you could tighten the loose tire by driving wedges between it and the wheel [it also helped to remove the wheel at night and soak it in a nearby stream]. At best though these were temporary solutions. A more permanent repair had to wait until the train arrived at a facility with a blacksmith shop. So far that had happened exactly once in the previous twelve weeks. But, fortunately they had just such an opportunity dead ahead for, on the 14th of August, the train arrived at Fort Bridger.

This post was the first in the West built specifically to service the emigrant trade. Its founders, Jim Bridger and his partner Louis Vasquez, had been mountain-men for twenty years when they came to the realization that the trade as they had known it was coming to an end. They were aware of the increased interest in

Oregon and rightly judged that the trickle of emigrants who had so far crossed the continent to go there would eventually become a flood. So they chose a spot ideally positioned to attract road-weary travelers and in the spring of 1843 began building a fort; they finished it just in time to service the Great Migration.

Few, if any, men then alive knew the country better than Bridger and Vasquez and that was evident in their choice of the post's location. At the head of a long valley, Blacks Fork of the Green River splits into several streams that flow independently across many miles of level terrain before rejoining. The courses divide the valley into several islands and on the western-most of these stood Fort Bridger. The cool, clear, tree-lined streams and fields of waving grass combined to provide a beautiful setting; an oasis surrounded by a harsh wilderness.

In December of 1843 Bridger, who could neither read nor write, dictated a letter to a firm in St. Louis looking for support for his enterprise. He had this to say about his prospects and the emigrants he had just seen:

I have established a small fort, with a blacksmith shop and a supply of iron in the road of the emigrants on Black's Fork of Green River, which promises fairly. In coming out they are generally well supplied with money, but by the time they get here they are in need of all kinds of supplies, horses, provision, smithwork, etc.

Based on the emigrant's diaries, Bridger apparently had not yet put in much in the way of supplies. Overton Johnson remarked that his group stayed there three days but left to go hunting, "as our stock of provisions was nearly exhausted." John Boardman, with the California Company, said they planned, "to stay 10 or 15 days to make meat, but what our disappointment to learn that the Sioux and Cheyenne had been there, run off all the buffalo, killed 3 Snake Indians, and stolen 60 horses."

So, Fort Bridger, like Fort Laramie, proved to be a big

disappointment to the emigrants. Especially since they had to leave one of their members there. On August 15th, three year-old Catherine, the daughter of Mr. & Mrs. Miles Cary, died after a short illness.

II

From Bridger, the emigrant train traveled due west along a creek called the Muddy through barren country completely destitute of grass except a little along the creek. Jim Nesmith called this the worst stretch they had yet seen. His opinion may have been prejudiced, however, since the wagon he accompanied capsized in crossing the Muddy. That accident, he said:

> . . . *[threw] all the loading into the water and wet all our clothing, blankets also. Our flour we saved without any material injury. After an hour's wading in water and mud waist deep, we succeeded in getting everything out.*

From the head of the Muddy the Company crossed a steep divide to the Bear River, which flows due north some forty miles or so from where the emigrants reached it and then at just about the current Wyoming border veers northwest into today's Idaho. After another forty or forty-five miles, it takes a sharp hairpin turn around a mountain and begins flowing south until it reaches the Great Salt Lake in Utah.

The crossing of the divide to the Bear was difficult — William Newby called it, "The worst road we hav had, sidling, hilley & deepe gull[i]es," — but the valley they now entered was worth the effort. Peter Burnett described the river as clear and beautiful with an abundance of good fish and plenty of ducks and geese.

The Company planned a leisurely week to pass through this garden spot, using the time to recruit their stock on the lush grass and prepare themselves for the barren Snake River Valley that lay ahead.

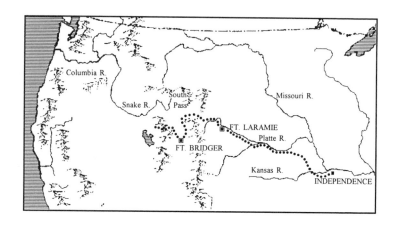

The Bear River Valley

Week Fourteen: August 20 - August 26

T he Bear River, the next stop on the journey west for the Oregon Emigrating Company, was, according to Pierson Reading, "a stream about 20 yards wide, three to five feet deep, rapid and running N.W. to a beautiful valley from five to six miles wide." He further noted that the company had now left the buffalo range, but the emigrant hunters compensated by bagging several elk and deer while anglers took the opportunity to catch a few trout. (The taste of trout was a welcome new experience for them as that fish did not exist east of the Rockies.) They also had their first opportunity to savor bear meat. John Boardman found it, "good and fat."

Diarist Overton Johnson and his group trailed the main body by nearly a week as they entered the Bear Valley (they had delayed to hunt, without success, in the Uinta Mountains at the head of the river). He described the valley as one to eight miles wide with good soil, excellent grass, and flax that grew spontaneously in large quantities. He reported, however, a sparsity of trees, only a few cottonwoods scattered along the river. Always interested in game, he wrote, "These streams abound with a fine fish called the Mountain Trout. We found wild Goats and large flocks of Geese, Ducks and Cranes, but they had been so much hunted by the Emigrants, that it was almost impossible to kill any of them."

An additional commentator on the Bear Valley that summer of 1843, was a distinguished observer who left the following word-picture of what he saw:

Crossing, in the afternoon, the point of a narrow spur, we descended into a beautiful bottom, formed by a lateral valley, which presented a picture of home beauty that went directly to our hearts. The edge of the wood, for several miles along the river, was dotted with the white covers of emigrant wagons, collected in groups at different camps, where the smokes were rising lazily from the fires, around which the women were occupied in preparing the evening meal, and the children playing in the grass; and herds of cattle grazing about in the bottom, had an air of quiet security, and civilized comfort, that made a rare sight for the traveller in such a remote wilderness."

The witness of this idyllic scene was John Charles Frémont. Frémont, with a party of thirty-nine men, had left Independence, Missouri on the 29th of May, seven days after the departure of the Great Migration. His mission was to complete an assignment he had begun the year before, requiring him to map the entire route to Oregon for future emigrations. In 1842 he had progressed as far as the South Pass. This year, he began by scouting out the territory in the vicinity of the head waters of the South Platte River to see if another route farther south existed. After determining that no feasible wagon route existed there, he crossed over to the South Pass and began following the emigrant train. He did not catch up with them until the Bear River Valley, but frequently intersected with them from there on to the Columbia.

The emigrants also received visitors from a tribe of Indians known as the Snake or Shoshone. Except for natives encamped at Forts Laramie and Bridger, these were the first Indians they had seen since they left Pawnee country. Pierson Reading, a reliable observer, found the Snakes quite friendly and willing to trade, "selling horses for blankets, knives, etc." Theodore Talbot, a traveler with Frémont's party, said of these Indians:

> We found them very friendly, quiet, honest and inoffensive. . . . . The Shoshonees or Snakes have very fine horses, they are of different breed to the generality of Indian horses. The trappers prefer Snake Indians and Snake horses before any race of men or horses in the world.

Accompanying the Indian visitors was a legendary trapper who had married into the tribe and had lived with them for years. He was known as Peg-Leg Smith. According to mountain-man lore, Smith received his nickname after amputating his own leg with a Bowie knife following a severe accident.

As the trains ambled slowly through the lush Bear Valley, they came upon two marvels that have long since disappeared because of damming of the River. The first, called Beer Springs by mountain-men and Lt. Frémont, the emigrants identified as Soda Springs. According to Jim Nesmith:

> . . . the greatest curiosity in this part of the country are the soda springs, which boil up in level ground and sink again. They are quite numerous and have exactly the taste of soda water without the syrup.

The restrained Mr. Reading tasted the water, "and found it quite palatable," while young William Newby said, "these springs bile up & dont run off. Appears to go a way as it biles. The water tasts like sody after it is done buyling."

Frémont wrote that voyageurs and trappers called them Beer Springs because, "in the midst of their rude and hard lives [they] are fond of finding some fancied resemblance to the luxuries they rarely have the fortune to enjoy."

The next attraction, in nearly the same area, was Steamboat Springs. Theodore Talbot described how it got its name:

Here the water bursts out of a hole six or eight inches in diameter, at intervals of half a second, and is thrown up, occasionally to the height of ten feet. The water is very warm, its deposits of a reddish color. Around this spring are several holes, to which if the ear be applied, a sound is heard exactly resembling that of a high pressure steam engine in full operation.

(Newby said it was as warm as dish water and "roars like a belles [bellows].")

The companies left the Bear Valley at the point where the river begins its hairpin curve towards the Great Salt Lake and traveled twenty miles to the first stream that brought them into the Columbia River drainage system, the Portneuf, a tributary of the Snake. After fourteen weeks and nearly twelve hundred miles they were entering the last leg of their ordeal but just beginning their most severe test.

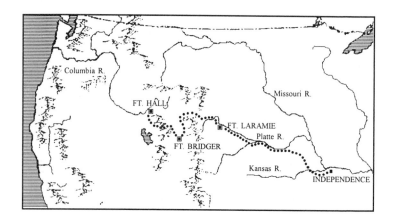

CHAPTER SEVENTEEN

Fort Hall

Week Fifteen: August 27 - September 2

O n Sunday, August 27, the first wagons of the Great Migration rolled up alongside the palisaded walls of Fort Hall, the third fort they had visited along the trail from the frontier of Missouri. This Hudson's Bay Company trading post, which Theodore Talbot described as, "a small and rather ill constructed Fort, built of 'Dobies,'" stood a few miles north of the mouth of the Portneuf on the Snake River in what is now the state of Idaho. Though then in possession of the British, at one time the fort had been the only American outpost in the entire Oregon country.

Its history began when Nathaniel J. Wyeth, a young man with great ambition but terrible luck, arrived in the Far West in 1832. He had come to launch a plan conceived while he was engaged in

Fort Hall (interior)

the ice business back in New England. Wyeth wanted to re-institute the old Astorian scheme of combining the beaver trade with maritime activity on the Pacific Coast. Deviating from Astor slightly because of the near extinction of sea otters, he intended to combine a salmon fishery with the collection of beaver skins. Like Astor, he intended to ship both the fish and the furs out of a post on the Columbia.

Unfortunately, his frustrations began immediately when the supply ship he had sent around the horn to meet with him in the Oregon country sank without ever arriving there. Discouraged but not defeated, he headed back to the states to seek additional financial backing.

During his trip to the West, he had attended the summer rendezvous and was appalled at the prices the mountain-men were paying for supplies out of St. Louis. So, on his return home in 1833, he stopped by that year's rendezvous and convinced several of the leading trappers to sign a contract with him. In exchange for their business he agreed to provide them with supplies in 1834 on a far more equitable basis than had been done in the past.

Fort Hall (Replica)

Again, however, misfortune dogged his every move. He secured the backing he desired all right, bought a caravan worth of supplies, and headed West. But he was a young greenhorn in an old and vicious business. He arrived at rendezvous to find that the regular trading firm had beaten him there by a week and by using leverage in the form of outstanding debts had forced the trappers to accept the same old terms in exchange for pelts, regardless of their agreement with the newcomer. Naturally the actions of what he called a majority of scoundrels devastated Wyeth and he vowed to get even. He said, in effect, "you think you have your own little Eden out here but I am going to roll a rock into your garden."

He moved his supplies farther west to the Snake River and began construction of the post that he named Fort Hall in honor of one of his financial backers. This would be his "rock." He planned to dispose of his goods at a price that would entice trappers away from future dealings at rendezvous and provide them with an opportunity to trade year-round instead of just in the summer.

Once more, though, he misjudged, for now he was intruding

upon the exclusive domain of the Hudson's Bay Company. Although, on paper, the Oregon country was open to both American and British subjects, in fact trappers had long ago conceded everything west of the Rockies to the Hudson's Bay Company. And that powerful firm did not like competition. So, in retaliation to Wyeth's move, they built their own post on the Snake at the mouth of the Boise River, and began undercutting the newcomer across the board.

Within two years Wyeth gave up the battle. His salmon fishery had failed to prosper, his beaver trading fort was a flop, and he was broke. He sold out to the Hudson's Bay Company and returned to New England, never to be heard from again.

Even with Wyeth out of the way, though, the HBC continued to operate both Fort Hall and Fort Boise as trading posts and collection points for their own trappers; so, each site was well entrenched when the new business of emigrant trade began.

The Oregon emigrants of 1843 received fine treatment from the man in charge at Fort Hall, Richard Grant. Pierson Reading said, "his kindness and hospitality to the emigrants are almost extreme, and it appears to give him much pleasure to have it in his power to serve them." Yet, there was only so much he could do. The demand for provisions quickly exhausted his stock of supplies even though he sold them at what Jim Nesmith called exorbitant prices. Once again the Great Migration found that no one was prepared to accommodate such a large number of people.

Late arrivals suffered the most; nearly everything had disappeared from the shelves by the time they got there. Further, Grant angered some of the stragglers by holding back a portion of his inventory for the benefit of his own personnel as a hedge against the oncoming winter. The group bound for California became especially incensed and two men from that train threatened the commander with violence if he refused to sell them supplies. Since a few of Frémont's men happened to be near the post at the time and promised to back the emigrants, there was little that Grant the Britisher could do but give in.

Ill feelings between the British and Americans at that point in history were nothing new. The nations had fought two wars against each other in less than sixty years and another one threatened over the question of Oregon. Though the Hudson's Bay Company served the emigrants well, it was difficult for the Americans to forget the politics of the situation.

Over the years Fort Hall became the principal point where trains headed for Oregon divided from those going to California. That split occurred in 1843 as well, though the California-bound train of that year followed the Snake River for a longer distance than future trains would do. Captain Gantt, the guide, Colonel Martin, the leader who had succeeded Burnett as commander of the Oregon Emigrating Company, and Pierson Reading, the Great Migration's most reliable diarist, now left the main body and joined the company headed for California.

Daniel Richardson of Franklin County, Missouri, also left the Company at Fort Hall. He died on the last day of August leaving a wife and two children to struggle on without him.

And struggle they would; for, as Peter Burnett expressed it, the Company now arrived at the most critical period in the entire adventure — emigrant wagons had never before gone beyond Fort Hall. The leaders consulted with Grant and that man advised, as he had consistently done with earlier emigrants, that they should not attempt to move their wagons any farther. Burnett remembered him stating that, "while he would not say it was impossible for us Americans to make the trip in our wagons, he could not himself see how it could be done."

Doctor Whitman took a different view. He assured Burnett and others that this migration differed from earlier ones in that it had sufficient manpower to overcome any obstacle. "We could succeed," Burnett quoted him as saying, "and [he] encouraged and aided us with every means in his power."

Whitman versus Grant, American versus British, success versus failure, which would it be? Burnett spoke for nearly everyone when he said, "We fully comprehended the situation, but we never faltered in our inflexible determination to accomplish this trip." Although some emigrants did leave their wagons at Fort Hall and switch to pack animals, the majority did not. Despite the discouragement, the risks, and the weariness, the experiment would go on. These people were not quitters.

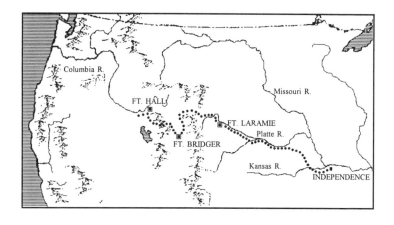

CHAPTER EIGHTEEN

The First Wagons West

Week Sixteen: September 3 - September 9

During the first week in September the Oregon Emigrating Company rolled along the Snake River towards a place in history. Their's were the first emigrant wagons ever to travel beyond Fort Hall. Men who knew the territory said it could not be done, but they had set their minds to taking wagons all the way to the Willamette Valley. That is the true spirit of pioneering, breaking new trails and doing what others less determined would not attempt. Others had made it possible for them to get this far. Now it was their turn to set the example for those who were sure to follow.

The history of wagon travel west of the Missouri began only thirteen years earlier when another group of stubborn men also decided to attempt what had never been done before. In 1830, William Sublette, Jedediah Smith, and David Jackson decided to deviate from the normal practice of moving supplies to rendezvous with a pack train of mules and chose instead to conduct an experiment using wheels. They left St. Louis on April 10th with ten wagons drawn by five mules each, two Dearborns pulled by one mule apiece (a Dearborn was a light passenger wagon), and eighty men mounted on mules.

The caravan crossed the state of Missouri and then followed nearly the same trail the Great Migration used across Kansas to the Platte and on to the Rockies. They arrived at that year's rendezvous at the head of the Wind River (west-central Wyoming) on July 16th. After trading for the year's harvest of beaver pelts they returned to Missouri by the same route they had come, leaving the mountains on August 4th and arriving in St. Louis on October 10th. All ten wagons made it each way, but the Dearborns were left in Wyoming.

The three partners were so proud of their accomplishment that they wrote a letter to the Secretary of War, John Eaton, describing the experience. Their letter included the statement, "This is the first time the wagons ever went to the Rocky mountains; and the ease and safety with which it was done prove the facility of communicating over land with the Pacific Ocean."

Their expedition stopped short of crossing the South Pass since the rendezvous was held east of there, but the next wagons west did cross over that crucial section of the continental divide. These wheels belonged to Captain Benjamin Bonneville.

Bonneville is somewhat of an enigma in Western history. He was an ordinary Army officer who suddenly had the wherewithal to take a two years leave of absence (which he overstayed by more than a year without punishment) and launch an ambitious fur-trading scheme that could afford to employ more than one hundred men and yet never made a dime. Some historians have suggested that the entire episode was simply a cover for a spying operation against the Hudson's Bay Company in Oregon and the

Mexicans in California.

Regardless, the Captain did take twenty wagons across the South Pass in 1832, and continued on to the Green River where he built a fort to serve as his headquarters. (He named his fort Bonneville, but the fur-trappers called it Fort Nonsense.) Though no record exists to indicate what happened to the wagons after they reached the Green River, presumably they rotted away with the Fort.

The next important episode in the history of wagon movement west occurred in 1836 when Marcus Whitman, Henry Spalding, and their wives headed to the Oregon country to establish their missions. The missionary party left civilization with two wagons, one a light Dearborn and the other a regular farm wagon and, as was the custom of the times, they traveled with the rendezvous caravan. The difficulty of moving wheeled vehicles over the roadless terrain convinced them to abandon the heavier farm wagon at Fort Laramie. There they loaded their supplies on pack animals but kept the lighter Dearborn drawn by two mules.

Although the women rode in the light wagon occasionally, that convenience alone could not explain Henry and Marcus' determination to keep it. In fact, Narcissa Whitman became exasperated with her new husband's persistence in wrestling the obvious burden across ravines, gullies, streams and rivers and dealing with frequent upsets. On a day when it turned over twice, she confided in her journal that she was not at all surprised as, "it was a greater wonder that it was not turning a somerset continually." She added, "It is not very grateful to my feelings to see him wearing out with such excessive fatigue. . . in his laborious attempt to take the wagon over."

Just a few days later, two days before arriving at Fort Hall, she experienced a moment of jubilation when one of the axle-trees broke, but the joy soon turned to tight-lipped resignation when the men turned the wagon into a cart and continued on. She wrote; "They are so resolute and untiring in their efforts they will probably succeed [in taking it through]."

124

Beyond Fort Hall, however, the road became rougher and rougher until finally even the hard-headed Marcus Whitman had to admit defeat. Reluctantly he left the jury-rigged cart at Fort Boise. Narcissa generously recorded the reason without gloating, "Perhaps you will wonder why we have left the wagon, having taken it so nearly through. Our animals are failing, and the route in crossing the Blue Mountains is said to be impassable for it."

Despite his failure, Doctor Whitman could console himself with the knowledge that a new milestone in wagon travel towards the Columbia had been reached. He surely had this experience in mind when he convinced the Oregon Emigrating Company that with their large numbers they could accomplish what he had not.

He also knew that only three years earlier the first wagons ever to reach the Columbia River from the frontier of Missouri had passed through this same country. That adventure began when three missionary couples, each with their own wagon, headed for Oregon by following the fur-trade caravan to rendezvous. As it turned out they were the last ever to do so. With the fur-trade in decline, the trading companies decided to discontinue support for the annual trading fair. One of the most famous institutions of the old West, the rendezvous, ceased to exist after 1840.

While at the last rendezvous, the missionaries sought out a guide to pilot them as far as Fort Hall en route to their final destination in the Willamette Valley. They began negotiations with a trapper known as "Black" Harris, but that man's fee was so steep it would have taken all the resources they had to hire him. As word got out about how they were being treated, another trapper, Robert (Doc) Newell, volunteered to lead them for far less. Doc had concluded that the old fur-trapping days would never return, anyway, so he might as well move to the Valley himself and commence farming.

Once the deal was struck, Black Harris became so incensed over being undercut that he tried to kill Doc by firing at him from a distance of about 80 yards. Years later, in his reminiscences, Newell said two things surprised him about that affair with his old comrade: One, that Harris would shoot at him, and secondly, that he missed.

Anyway, with his scalp still intact, Doc talked two of his friends into joining him on the adventure. So, with their mountain families, as well as a Hudson's Bay Company employee named Francis Ermatinger, they all set out from the Green River to pilot the missionaries to their destination.

The party reached Fort Hall in sixteen days without mishap, although the draft animals had become so wasted by then that they could not continue. The experience convinced the missionaries to continue the remainder of the way on horseback. Since they had little in the way of resources, they persuaded Newell to accept their wagons as payment for his services.

Now stuck with three wagons, Newell had to figure how to get them to the Willamette Valley. He rid himself of one of them by selling it to Ermatinger for use at Fort Hall. Next, he hired his fur-trapping buddy, Joe Meek, to drive another, and then loaded his family in the third to head for a new career.

As Newell and Meek prepared to leave, Caleb Wilkins, the third trapper who had traveled with them from rendezvous, obtained a wagon of his own at the Fort and joined them. The motley caravan consisted of three wagons pulled by mules, driven by three ex-mountain-men, and loaded with their Indian wives and half-breed children.

They probably started out in high spirits. After all wagon travel was quite a luxury to a mountain-man's family. But the trip across the lava plain of southern Idaho turned out to be far more than any of them had bargained for. In his reminiscences, Newell wrote:

In a few days we began to realize the difficulty of the task before us, and found that the continual crashing of the sage under our wagons, which was in many places higher than the mules' backs, was no joke. Seeing our animals begin to fail, we began to light up, finally threw away our wagon beds, and were quite sorry we had undertaken the job.

Eventually, however, the three friends struggled through to Whitman's mission near Walla Walla with nothing left of their wagons but the running gear. Marcus Whitman made them welcome and prophesied that, despite the difficulties, Newell would never regret having brought the wagons that far. "You have broken the ice," he said, "and when others see that wagons have passed they too will pass, and in a few years the valley will be full of our people."

That made a nice speech, but enough was enough. After resting their families, Newell and his friends continued on to the Willamette Valley by pack train.

By the next spring, though, Doc had second thoughts. He could see that a wagon would be an asset on his farm; so, he returned to the mission and brought one of the wagons on to the Valley by boat. Thus, shortly afterwards he could write in his journal:

This is to be remembered that I, Robert Newell, was the first who brought wagons across the Rocky Mountains and up to this 19th April, 1841, and have it at this time on my farm about 25 miles from Vancouver west.

Ironically, within a month after the historic wagon arrived at the farm on the Tualatin Plains, the first avowed emigration to the Pacific gathered outside of Independence, Missouri. That 1841 train took fourteen wagons as far as Fort Hall. The next year, eighteen wagons followed the same path and they, too, got no farther than the Hudson's Bay Post. But now the Great Migration of 1843 had determined to shatter the barrier. Every mile they could travel would make it that much easier for those who would come after them.

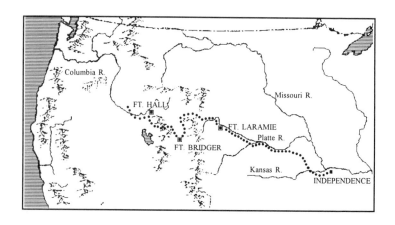

CHAPTER NINETEEN

The Snake River Plateau

Week Seventeen: Sept. 10 - Sept. 16

A fter leaving Fort Hall, the Oregon Emigrating Company rolled through some of the most difficult country they had yet encountered, the Snake River Plateau. Almost devoid of grass, the rough, rocky, lava plain yielded only sagebrush that grew to a height of three feet or more. And what sagebrush it was! Peter Burnett claimed they would have had to cut their way through if it had been any hardier. As it was they alternated the five or six leading wagons every few miles to spread the toil of breaking down and crushing the coarse stubble under the feet of the oxen and the wheels of their wagons.

The emigrants trailed along the south bank of the Snake, but most of the time they were a long way from the water. Over the ages the river had cut a chasm so deep that the stream was impossible to reach in many locations. Even when the terrain did allow access it still involved a long climb down a steep bluff. Theodore Talbot, described the country:

We camped for the night on a high basaltic cliff overhanging the river and some two hundred and eighty feet above it. To reach the water we have to follow a path nearly a mile long winding down the face of the cliffs to the River side. Snake River, along here for miles, is walled in by high, perpendicular, basaltic bluffs, and in the parlance of the country, is said to run through a "canon". The river is thus some hundred feet below the general level of the country, which consists of barren rock partly covered with sand and patches of absinthe. You may almost ride up to the brink of the chasm through which the river flows without being aware of its existence.

William Newby, too, wrote of a camp on a high bluff above the river where they had to travel one mile to reach water. John Boardman's diary tells of a man named Prigg who attempted to ride a mule down to the water, "The saddle slipped over the mules head and down the mountain at a furious rate rolled poor Prigg." Another man named White lost an ox when it fell down a bluff and suffered a broken neck.

The difficulty in reaching water was not the only problem now confronting the emigrants, there was also a lack of adequate forage for the animals. Day after day John Boardman would write: "Little grass; Little grass; Good camp. Little water. Country sand, rock and sage; Nooned with no grass; camped without grass; and so on and so on. Finally, during these trials, he became uncharacteristically philosophic, painting a lovely word-picture of his life on the trail:

How seldom as this evening comes around do I think of the happy hours I have had on this day with those I love, and whose memory I hold most dear. And why —, the only, and good reason is — a person is thinking of the tedious and tiresome journey — of his animals (as all depends on them), whether they may not be stolen or get away, perhaps turn their packs and lose part of the things, or break something; and when near camping time, he is all anxiety to get good grass, wood and water. As soon as camp is struck, then get wood, make fire, cook and eat, then mend pants, moccasins, pack-saddles, cruppers, lash-rope, girths, &c, or alter his packs, as one too heavy and hurts the mule's back. Then comes making bed, and by that time, one only thinks of enjoying repose, and so sweet and undisturbed that he cannot even dream of his native land or those he loves.

John Charles Frémont, following the trail of the emigrants, sympathized with their plight. In his official report he said:

. . . on the line of road along the barren valley of the Upper Columbia [Snake], there does not occur, for a distance of nearly three hundred miles to the westward, a fertile spot of ground sufficiently large to produce the necessary quantity of grain, or pasturage enough to allow even a temporary repose to the emigrants. . . . It was now no longer possible, as in our previous journey, to travel regularly every day and find at any moment a convenient place for repose at noon, or a camp at night; but the halting places were now generally fixed along the road by the nature of the country, at places where, with water, there was a little scanty grass.

As if the terrain did not provide enough problems, many of the emigrants were running frightfully short of provisions. John Shively said that after leaving Fort Hall he had a gallon of unbolted flour and about the same of dried service berries. That had to last him eight hundred miles. Fortunately, he was able to trade with the Indians at Salmon Falls for dried salmon. This he

Snake River Crossing

pulverized with a spoonful of flour to make a soup. That provided his breakfast and dinner. For lunch he had the berries.

Like Shively, many emigrants took advantage of the chance to trade with the Indians who clustered at several spots beside Salmon Falls catching salmon. Overton Johnson identified the location as being 139 miles beyond American Falls. Here, the fish became entrapped since a few miles beyond they encountered another falls they could not ascend. He wrote, "the Indians take immense quantities of Salmon, which they cut into thin slices, dry in the sun, and afterwards pack them in grass cases." Theodore Talbot said, "The river on this side and all the islands are lined with shanties and black with Indians all occupied in catching or drying salmon."

The main article of trade with the tribes was clothing. Frémont, in the wake of the emigrants, noted:

> *We now very frequently saw Indians . . . very many of them were oddly and partially dressed in overcoat, shirt, waistcoat, or pantaloons, or whatever article of clothing they had been able to procure in trade from the emigrants; for we had now entirely quitted the country where hawks' bells, beads, and*

vermilion were the current coin, and found that here only useful articles, and chiefly clothing, were in great request.

Overton Johnson also noted a sad peculiarity about the Snake Indians:

The native along Snake River live principally upon fish and roots, and are the fattest, most depraved, and degraded creatures anywhere to be found among the dregs of human nature. We have been told that during the Salmon season they become as fat as pigs, and in the winter so poor and feeble that they frequently die from actual starvation.

The Indians were not the only ones who had been reckless with plenty. Many of the Oregon emigrants might well have starved if the people they looked down on had not been willing to trade with them.

Some thirty miles from Salmon Falls the Snake River widened out into a bay in which there were two shallow islands. Here, the emigrants decided to cross over to the north side. William Newby wrote that they drove their wagons 100 yards across the stream to the first island and then about 75 yards more to the second. From the second island they had to chain the wagons together to make the final crossing. At that point the water was ten inches up the wagon beds in the deepest places. The total crossing covered about 900 yards.

The current in the final section of the crossing was quite strong; so, while fording, they placed two of their heavier wagons abreast of each other to oppose the current in the deepest channel. Most of those who followed the leaders made it across without incident. One man, however, decided he would do things his own way.

Sarah Owens said this independent cuss, an Englishman named Miles Eyers, "was a very unsocial and disagreeable man; he usually camped a quarter of a mile away from the company," According to her eyewitness account:

Mr Eyers would not heed the protestations of the company,
but persisted in driving his fine mule team in by himself. The
mules soon became unmanageable and turned upstream. Soon
Mr. Eyers disappeared from sight, lost his life and every thing
he had.

Another witness, Edward Lenox, called Eyers an old man of
sixty and said that when his mules began to get into trouble
another man, C. M. Stringer about age thirty, attempted to help
and lost his life, too.

Fortunately, Eyers' wife and family had became so frightened
by his stubbornness that they begged to be ferried by others and
reached the far shore safely. To add to their tragedy, however, the
bodies were never recovered and, since Eyers had all of his money
strapped around his waist, his death left his family not only
bereaved but destitute as well.

At this same crossing, John Stoughton claimed that only the
intervention of Marcus Whitman prevented the addition of his
name to the toll:

Dr. Whitman saved my life in crossing Snake River. We had
chained about ten wagons together. There were two islands,
and we had to cross from one to the other. In crossing Dr.
Whitman rode beside the wagon I had charge of, which was
the hindmost wagon. He kept punching the cattle in the side
to keep them from the deep water. The current was very
strong and came against the bank with terrible force. Before
we were across I had got so far below that my horse lunged
into deep water and Doctor Whitman, seeing the dangerous
position I was in, wheeled around and left the cattle to pull
the wagons out and grabbed my horse by the bridle, hollering
'let go the reins.' He pulled him so that we reached the
island in safety.

For two days after the Oregon Emigrating Company and the

Cow Column crossed the Snake, a steady rain fell, the river rose, and straggling companies found it impossible to cross. Overton Johnson, for example, attempted to ford the same spot and found it too deep. He continued on down the south side of the Snake through country he called "the most rugged, desert and dreary country, between the western borders of the United States and the shores of the Pacific."

John Boardman, too, tried the island crossing and found the final stretch impossible even with pack mules. Like Johnson he was forced to continue down the south side of the Snake where he described what he saw as, "Bad road. Sage and sand. Plenty of dirty Indians."

About eight miles after crossing the Snake, the main body of emigrants reached an area of decent grazing and laid over for a day to allow their stock to recruit themselves. From that camp they proceeded past another curiosity of the trail, called by Peter Burnett, "the Boiling Spring."

Luckily, William Newby (who called it "Hot Springs Creek"), provided another one of his patented descriptions: "We past the hot spring in 2 miles of whir we struck the creek. Thare is 3 springs that run off very pirty that is hot enough to scald a hog or coock a egg in 5 minits. It smoaks as it runs off."

From the springs, the trail headed towards the Boise River. Grazing had improved to the extent that Newby now called it "tollerable," though he wrote as well, "I mention all the creek & grass &c as this is the difficulty in taraveling through this country. I will say from Fort Hawl to the Bliew Mountains."

At least they did have one break coming up, they were nearing another fort.

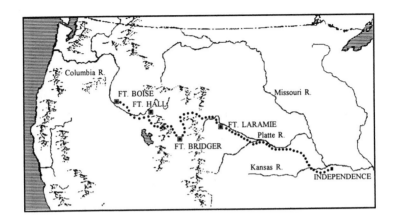

CHAPTER TWENTY

Fort Boise

Week Eighteen: Sept. 17 - Sept. 23

O n September 18, the Oregon Emigrating Company reached the Boise River (meaning Wooded River in French) and two days later pulled up next to Fort Boise. They had traveled three weeks and 274 miles from Fort Hall to get there. (They were 1519 miles from Missouri).

Since leaving Fort Hall they had labored through some of the roughest terrain of the entire trip. And the effort had begun to take its toll. The men were tired, cranky, and impatient. (Just the week prior there had been an incident in camp in which one man stabbed another.) For the last three weeks they had had to contend with little water or grass for their teams and dwindling provisions for their families. Many must have cursed the day they decided to

135

Fort Boise

go to Oregon.

The stay at Fort Boise did not ease their discomfort. Once again the needs of such a large group placed an impossible burden on a small outpost. The early wagons quickly exhausted all available supplies, leaving stragglers with nothing. John Boardman, who at this point decided to go to Oregon instead of California, recorded in his diary, "the Oregon company had bought all that could be spared, and many of the company almost starved or suffering for want of provisions. No flour, meat, rice or sugar."

The function of Fort Boise, like Fort Hall, was that of a fur-trading post. There were no facilities to service emigrant travel. The Hudson's Bay Company had established the post in 1834, the same year Nathaniel Wyeth built Fort Hall. As mentioned earlier, Wyeth had alarmed the Company by moving into their exclusive territory and they countered his effort by building a post of their own.

The man in charge at Boise when the Oregon emigrants arrived, Francois Payette, had come to the country with John Jacob Astor's ill-fated supply ship the *Tonquin* in 1811. When the Astorians found themselves forced to give up their enterprise on the Columbia in 1812, he chose not to return to the United States but, instead, joined the rival Canadians as a fur-trapper. The 1843 travelers found him "a very agreeable old French gentleman," (Jim Nesmith) and "exceedingly polite, courteous and hospitable" (Theodore Talbot).

The fort was quite small. It had 15 foot adobe walls that surrounded a parallelogram only about 100 feet square. It stood on the south bank of the Boise River, near where that stream emptied into the Snake. To reach their destination, then, the emigrants would once again have to cross the Snake River.

Fortunately, the second crossing went smoothly. Jim Nesmith said the water (on September 20th) was only "about four feet six inches deep." (The Cow Company crossed three days later and Newby said, though the ford was better here than the earlier Snake River crossing, it was about 8-10 inches deeper. Their company chained the wagons together and drove straight across an estimated 600 yards.)

After crossing the Snake, the trains left the river temporarily and trailed without incident about twelve miles north-west to the Malheur River. Twenty-two miles from the Malheur they once again struck the Snake River but now for the last time at a place they called "Farewell Bend." They were now on their way to a new and difficult test — the Burnt River Canyon.

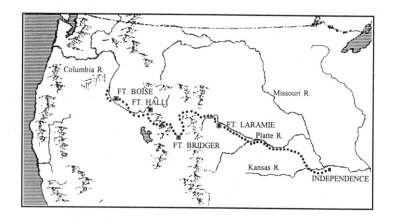

CHAPTER TWENTY-ONE

The Burnt River Canyon

Week Nineteen: Sept. 24 - Sept. 30

I n one of the cruel ironies of the Oregon trail, the most difficult stretches occurred when the emigrants were least prepared to handle them. The pioneers of 1843 soon learned it was no accident that emigrant wagons had never traveled farther than Fort Hall.

Consider for a moment how much easier the trail would have been had it run in the opposite direction. If the emigrants had traveled from the Willamette Valley to Missouri, they would have tackled the Columbia River, the Blue Mountains, the Burnt River Canyon, and the Snake River Plateau while they were fresh and eager. That way, the wide open prairie would have come at the end, when they were mentally and physically exhausted and in desperate need of relief. But, of course, had that been the case we

138

would not be marveling at their experience 150 years later.

Anyway, as the Oregon Emigrating Company began their nine-teenth week on the trail, they left the Snake River at Farewell Bend. Once again the experiences of earlier fur-traders helped them make that decision.

In December of 1811, John Jacob Astor's overland party led by Wilson Price Hunt had traversed this same country as they struggled to reach the mouth of the Columbia River. Unfortunately for them, they attempted to follow the Snake River north. Their experience taught all future white men not to make that mistake. The river is impassable that way. It roars for miles through a canyon of sheer cliffs over rapids so treacherous that only modern jet boats and inflatable rafts are capable of negotiating them. Further, the land on either side is so mountainous that it is also impossible to follow. Today the entire stretch bears the descriptive label: Hell's Canyon.

At first glance the Oregon emigrants thought the alternative route equally impassable. Less than a half day's journey from their last sight of the Snake, the wagon-train entered the Burnt River Canyon. The river itself (also known as the Brule), was hardly more than a creek according to Peter Burnett, but it meandered through mountainous country full of timber that they had neither the time nor force to remove. John Charles Frémont's official report declared that the stream had cut a ravine rather than a valley, and the steep sides made for rough traveling, even for horsemen.

Jim Nesmith agreed, calling it, "the roughest country I ever saw." Burnett described the road as terrible, and William Newby chimed in with, "the worst road we hav had."

This was the first time the emigrants had to double teams to move their wagons. Sara Jane Hill recalled that sometimes it would take eight or nine yoke of oxen to pull an individual wagon over the steep ascents. Other times, she said, four or five men at a time would station themselves above the wagon and tug on ropes to keep it from tipping over.

William Newby described a typical day:

(September 27) We crawsed the river or creek I shall cawl it as it is a smawl stream. Dubeld teamed & crawsed the hill. It was a bout 3 quarters of a mile up & about the same down. Then we continued up the creek crawsing it some 8 or 10 times. Then passing through the hills whir you mite loock any way & it loocked impossible for waggeons to pass we past with out much difficulty. Incampments is ginerally good up this creek. Distance 12 miles.

Frémont came through several days after the emigrant train and said he had never seen a wagon road equally bad in the same space. He continued, "I noticed where one wagon had been overturned twice in a very short distance; and it was surprising to me that those wagons which were in the rear, and could not have had much assistance, got through at all."

Somehow, though, they all made it, covering twenty-five to thirty miles in four days. After such an ordeal they were entitled to a respite and they got it. Overton Johnson explained:

From the head of the Brule, we came next to the valley of Powder River. Here the aspect of the country changes rapidly. Leaving behind us the Sage and Sand, we find the hills and Mountains covered with Pines, and the little valleys along the Creeks and Rivers with excellent grass. This valley is about ten miles wide and thirty miles long, a large portion of which has a good soil. It is encircled by hills and Mountains.

Peter Burnett stood at the top of the last hill out of the dreadful Burnt River Canyon and could scarcely restrain himself as he wrote of what he saw:

140

. . . ranges of tall mountains, covered on the sides with magnificent forests of pine, the mountain tops being dressed in a robe of pure snow, and around their summits the dense masses of black clouds wreathed themselves in fanciful shapes, the sun glancing through the open spaces upon the gleaming mountains. We passed through some most beautiful valleys and encamped on the branch of the Powder River at the Lone Pine.

The Lone Pine! It had stood for untold decades as a solitary landmark for travelers through the surrounding plain. Just the year before, an emigrant diarist named Medorem Crawford had written, "The Tree is a large Pine stand[ing] in the midst of an immense plain intirely alone. It presented a truly singular appearance and I believe is respected by every traviler through this almost Treeless Country."

Sadly, Burnett and his group were the last ever to see that famous tree as nature intended it. On September 28th, as Burnett guided his wagon-team down into the valley he used the tree as a landmark:

Many teams had passed on before me, and at intervals, as I drove along, I would raise my head and look at that beautiful green pine. At last, on looking up as usual, the tree was gone. I was perplexed for a moment to know whether I was going in the right direction. There was the plain, beaten wagon road before me, and I drove on until I reached the camp just at dark. That brave old pine, which had withstood the storms and snows of centuries, had fallen at last by the vandal hands of man. Some of our inconsiderate people had cut it down for fuel, but it was too green to burn. It was a useless and most unfortunate act. Had I been there in time I should have begged those woodmen to 'spare that tree.'

Among the first to miss it, besides the trailing emigrants, was

Frémont. He said:

> *From the heights we had looked in vain for a well known*
> *landmark on Powder River, which had been described to me*
> *by Mr. Payette [of Fort Boise] as l'arbre seul, (the lone tree;)*
> *and, on arriving at the river, we found a fine tall pine*
> *stretched on the ground, which had been felled by some*
> *inconsiderate emigrant axe.*

This episode took some of the luster off of the accomplishments of the Great Migration and served as a cruel reminder that progress has always been a two-edged sword. The cutting down of a single tree might seem insignificant, and it is. Nevertheless this act foreshadowed the twentieth century conflict over what one generation owes to another with respect to the natural environment. We have yet to find a satisfactory solution to that dilemma.

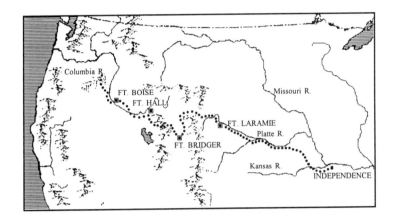

The Blue Mountain Crossing

Week Twenty: October 1 - October 7

F rom the time they entered the Powder River Valley, the Oregon Emigrating Company began to experience the Oregon they had expected to find when they left home. Here was land to delight the farmer. The next valley beyond the Powder, the Grande Ronde, especially impressed the members of the wagon train.

Peter Burnett described it as, "one of the most beautiful valleys in the world, embosomed among the Blue Mountains, which are covered with magnificent pines." Ninevah Ford said of the Grande Ronde, "there was a parley with the emigration as to whether we had better stop there or not. It was a beautiful country. They would have stopped and colonized it if we had had provisions."

In addition to the shortage of supplies, the extreme distance from the settlements in the Willamette Valley served to discourage any further thought of staying. In fact, it would be nearly two decades before the isolation of that garden spot could be overcome enough to attract permanent settlement. The '43 train did leave one of their members behind, though. On October 1, a lady identified as Mrs. Rubey died and was interred there.

The emigrant trains trailed ten miles across the lush valley, which Burnett estimated at one hundred miles in circumference, and then began climbing into the heavily forested Blue Mountains. Although the descent into the Grande Ronde had been rough and abrupt (Sara Jane Hill remembered, "it was the rockyest hill a wagon ever was taken over. There was a rock for every wheel from the hight of a half foot to a foot"), the ascent on the other side was even more difficult.

Curiously, the wagon trains had crossed the Rockies at South Pass without knowing when they had reached the divide, but the Blues, though by no means as rugged as the Rockies, provided no such convenience. For the first time they found themselves literally cutting a trail.

Peter Burnett, who had consistently shed the best light on every trial since they left Missouri, had to admit, "These hills were terrible." Ninevah Ford noted, "We camped many times in sight of our former night's camp. We found it very laborious and very hard cutting that Tamarisk timber with our dull axes that we had not ground since we left Missouri." William Newby described the timber as "so thick in meney places that you coldant see a man 10 steps."

The groves were indeed thick, so thick in fact that the emigrants found it difficult to keep track of their cattle, especially when the animals chose to lay down.

The emigrants cut a swath through the forest just wide enough for a wagon to pass, and did not bother to remove the stumps. About forty men did most of the cutting, with Nesmith receiving considerable praise for his efforts. In his own account, however, Jim merely remarked, "Trailed twelve miles to-day over bad roads, in many places timber to be cut. I went in advance and cut timber all day."

Another aspect of human nature revealed itself during this crossing, as noted by Ninevah Ford:

> *It devolved on some 40 persons to make that road. The lazy ones dropped back, not for the purpose of screening themselves, but to rest their cattle, so they stated, but we imputed it to their diffidence in regard to the work.*

In addition to the heavy work-load, the emigrants found themselves in the hands of an unusual pilot to guide them through the Blue Mountains. Ever since Fort Hall when John Gantt left the train to go to California, Marcus Whitman had assumed the role of guide. Upon entering the Grande Ronde Valley, however, he had received a message from his mission saying he was urgently needed and asking him to hurry home. So, the doctor turned his duties over to a faithful native from his mission named Stickus. It was this Cayuse Indian, then, who led the way across the Blues.

The emigrants had total confidence in Stickus, according to Ninevah Ford, "wherever he directed us to go, there we went, without searching for any other route." He continued, "He found us a pretty fair route for getting through. The Indian did not look about much, he was familiar with the ground."

Stickus was a Christian convert but spoke no English. Jim Nesmith remembered that he "succeeded by pantomime in taking us over the roughest wagon route I ever saw." During that episode Jim had occasion to dine with Stickus in his camp on what he supposed to be elk meat. He believed that to be its source because the Indian "held up his hands in a manner that indicated elk horns; but, after dinner, seeing the ears, tail and hoofs of a mule near camp, I became satisfied that what he meant to convey by his pantomime was ears not horns."

It took four days for the emigrants to cross the Blue Mountains and on the next to last day they suffered through a snow storm.

Though the storm passed quickly, it was a frightening reminder that winter was not far off and they were yet 300 miles from their destination. Fortunately, once they reached the top of the mountain the timber thinned out enough that they were able to complete the crossing without further interference from either weather or terrain.

At the western base of the mountain, near the Umatilla River, the emigrants encamped about three miles from a Cayuse Indian village. The natives proved eager to trade, offering vegetables in exchange for clothing. The Indian corn, peas, and potatoes provided a sumptuous feast for the eager emigrants who had not tasted fresh vegetables for months. Peter Burnett remarked, "I have never tasted a greater luxury than the potatoes we ate on this occasion."

These two incidents, the guidance of Stickus and bartering of vegetables, reveal once again the important role native Americans played in the success of the Great Migration. It is not surprising, however, that history has given such scant attention to such events since the emigrants themselves tended to emphasis the negative instead of the positive in their contacts with the natives. For instance, Jim Nesmith had this to say in his diary of the bartering that had occurred, "A few Cayuse Indians encamped close by us, of whom we purchased some corn and potatoes, and they in return, stole a tin cup from us. They possess great faculties for business of this sort."

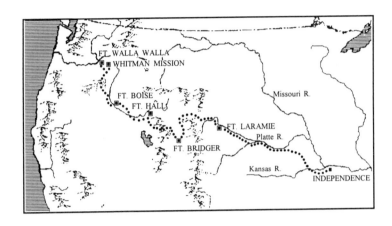

The Whitman Mission

Week Twenty-One: October 8 - October 14

A historian once compared the route of the Oregon Trail to a rope frayed on both ends; that is, emigrants began the odyssey from all points of the compass, followed a defined road from Missouri until they neared the beginning of settlement in Oregon, and then dispersed in the same manner as they had begun. In 1843 the final fraying began as the trains left the Umatilla River and approached Fort Walla Walla and the Whitman Mission.

The valley from the upper Umatilla to the Walla Walla is a broad expanse of gently rolling land without major obstruction. The natives of the area were peaceful, the route was apparent, and the need for mutual assistance was minimal; so, the emigrant wagons spread out until any semblance to a cohesive unit disap-

147

peared completely. With the end of the long journey in sight, the anxious no longer had any patience for dawdlers.

Leaving the Umatilla River, the '43 companies took two different routes. One trail led to the Hudson's Bay post near where the Walla Walla River empties into the Columbia. The alternative route led to the Whitman mission, also on the Walla Walla River, but twenty-five miles farther east. The need for repairs, supplies, or provisions dictated the path chosen.*

The mission route was the longest. Yet for families desperately short of food it was the only choice. Dr. Whitman had promised them an abundance of provisions would be available. He had not told them, however, what the cost would be; many found that to be a devious oversight.

From what Frémont described as, "one adobe house," at a place called Waiilatpu (meaning place of the rye grass), Dr. Whitman and his wife Narcissa had been ministering to the local Cayuse Indians since 1836. Tragically, though, they were fated to receive a martyr's death in 1847.

That year a wagon train carrying measles arrived at the mission and spread devastation among the natives who had no immunity to white men's diseases. The Cayuse leaders became convinced that Dr. Whitman was somehow responsible for the deaths among their people since his medicine cured whites but did nothing for them. They decided the epidemic must be part of a plot to steal their lands and give it to the white emigrants. Consequently, on the evening of November 29, 1847 several members of the tribe stormed into the mission house and exacted their revenge by slaughtering the doctor, his wife, and several others. (Eventually the death toll reached fifteen.)

---

* Later trains would eliminate the journey to the Walla Walla River completely. Instead they either followed down the Umatilla to its mouth or cut diagonally across to the Columbia.

Because the Whitman's paid with their lives for the assistance they gave to emigrant trains between 1843 and 1847, there has been considerable reluctance to suggest any charge of profiteering for their efforts. Nevertheless, several emigrants of 1843, uninfluenced by the future, felt victimized by the treatment they received. In his diary, William Newby described the situation:

We lay buy within 3 miles of Doct Whitmans, a mishionary astablishment, to git provision. . . . & the emigrants was much disapointed, as the Dr. had got them to come much out of there way with promices of provisions cheep, & was surprised by high prices that we had to pay for all we got: be[e]f 10 cts, pork 15 ct[s], potatoes $1.00, flour without bolting 7 c[ts].

Further, William Geiger, the agent in charge at the mission, encouraged many emigrants to swap their animals for fresh stock. Daniel Waldo became incensed over this suggestion and laid an additional charge on Whitman. That irascible emigrant claimed the Doctor purposely misled the emigrants in order to secure their livestock:

Whitman lied like hell. . . . He wanted my cattle and told me the grass was all burnt between this place and the Dalles. I told him I would try it anyhow. The first night I left [for] the Dalles I found the finest grass I ever saw, and it was good every night.

Sara Jane Hill stated that she and her husband traded two worn cows for "a beef," and Edward Lenox related a deal his father made at the mission as follows: "my father found it necessary to get new oxen, ours were so worn out, so we traded five oxen for two fresh new ones." Not a bad set of transactions for the mission considering that by the following year those jaded animals would be fully recruited and available for swap themselves.

John McClane admitted that the mission demanded two for one in trading cattle, but he found that a fair deal:

[Dr. Whitman] furnished the emigration with fat beef. Our cattle were all poor. He furnished them with fat steers some weighing 1500 lbs., the finest beef I ever saw. He furnished one of these big steers for two head of our cattle. If persons had not anything to trade with he would let them have the meat anyhow. He was one of those men who would divide the last thing he had.

Peter Burnett, often critical of his fellow travelers, also defended Whitman, stating, "The exhausting tedium of such a trip and the attendant vexations have a great effect upon the majority of men, especially upon those of weak minds. Men, under such circumstances, become childish, petulant, and obstinate." He continued:

I remember that while we were at the mission of Doctor Whitman, who had performed such hard labor for us, and was deserving of our warmest gratitude, he was most ungenerously accused by some of our people of selfish motives in conducting us past his establishment, where we could procure fresh supplies of flour and potatoes. This foolish, false, and ungrateful charge was based upon the fact that he asked us a dollar a bushel for wheat, and forty cents for potatoes. As our people had been accustomed to sell their wheat at from twenty to twenty-five cents, in the Western States, they thought the prices demanded by the doctor amounted to something like extortion, not reflecting that he had to pay at least twice as much for his own supplies of merchandise and could not afford to sell his produce as low as they did theirs at home. . . . I remember one case particularly, where an intimate friend of mine, whose supplies of food were nearly exhausted, refused to purchase, though

Fort Walla Walla

*urged to do so by me, until the wheat was all sold. The
consequence was that I had to divide provisions with him
before we reached the end of our journey.*

In further defense of the Whitmans, neither of them was at the
mission when the first emigrant wagons arrived. The doctor was
engaged in delivering a child at an outlying mission site and
Narcissa was at the Methodist mission at the Dalles. Whether the
situation would have been any different had they been there
instead of their agent will never be known. Obviously, though, the
circumstances did generate considerable hard feelings.

Not all of the emigrants took the longer route to the mission.
Many went directly to the Hudson's Bay post, Fort Walla Walla.
This fort, originally named Fort Nez Perce, had served fur-traders
for three decades since its erection by the Canadian rivals of the
Astorians.

John Charles Frémont arrived at the post while the emigrants
were there and left this description of the surrounding country:

*The post is on the bank of the Columbia, on a plain of bare
sands, from which the air was literally filled with clouds of*

151

dust and sand during one of the few days we remained here — this place being one of the several points on the river which are distinguished for prevailing high winds, which come from the sea. The appearance of the post and country was without interest, except that we here saw, for the first time, the great river on which the course of events for the last half-century has been directing attention and conferring historical fame.

The river is, indeed, a noble object, and has here attained its full magnitude. About nine miles above, and in sight from the heights about the post, is the junction of the two great forks which constitute the main stream — that on which we had been traveling from Fort Hall, and known by the names of Lewis' Fork, Shoshone, and Snake River; and the North Fork, which has retained the name of Columbia, as being the main stream.

(It is interesting to reflect at this point that had the Snake been navigable for rafts, the overland trail could have ended at Fort Hall. Pioneers in the past had always preferred to use rivers where possible.)

The Hudson's Bay man in charge at Fort Walla Walla in 1843 was Archibald McKinley of whom William Newby recorded, "two much cannot be said in his prase, tho the fort was poorly supplyed, yet all accommodations posable was extended."

Among those who by-passed Waiilatpu for the Fort were Jim Nesmith and three companions who found, "we could procure no eatables. Could only get a little tobacco, and Mr. McKinley, the manger was loath to part with that, in consequence of its being the Sabbath."

Needless to say Jim did not form a very high opinion of the place:

. . . near to the fort are sand banks not possessing fertility enough to sprout a pea, and in fact this is too much the case

with all the far-famed Walla Walla Valley. . . . If this is a fair specimen of Oregon, it falls far below the conceptions which I formed of the country. . . . The whole country looks poverty stricken.

He and his friends swapped their wagon and harness for a horse and concluded to pack the rest of the way to the Willamette Valley.

Many families, unwilling to load their children and belongings on horseback, nevertheless decided to abandon their wagons at the fort. Frémont noted while at Fort Walla Walla, the "broad expanse of the river here invites [the emigrants] to embark upon its bosom." He saw:

. . . a considerable body of the emigrants, under the direction of Mr. Applegate, a man of considerable resolution and energy, had nearly completed the building of a number of Mackinaw boats, in which they proposed to continue their further voyage down the Columbia.

As the boat-building efforts neared an end, Archibald McKinley invited Frémont and the heads of the emigration to a special dinner at the post. During the evening many must have expressed an appreciation for the civility, and congratulated each other that the worst was now behind them.

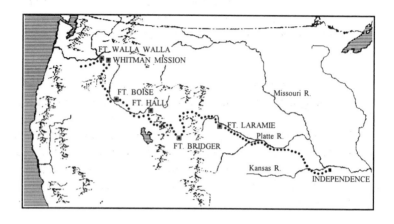

The Columbia River Indians

Week Twenty-Two: October 15 - October 22

At the Whitman mission and at Fort Walla Walla, the emigrants heard repeatedly that it would be impossible to take their wagons any farther west than the point where the Columbia River begins its break through the Cascade Range. From that place, called the Dalles, they were told that they would have to descend the Columbia by raft or boat to reach the Willamette Valley. Most of the emigrants determined to proceed by wagon, anyway, not trusting anyone to tell them how far they might get. And who could blame them. They had also heard that they could not go beyond Fort Hall.

After leaving the Walla Walla River, the wagon-trains followed along the Columbia until they were some 30 to 40 miles past the mouth of the Umatilla. There, the main stream began its flow through a land of high, broken bluffs that left no room for a road. By turning inland, a few miles to the south, according to Frémont, "The sand had disappeared, and the soil was good, and covered with excellent grass, although the surface was broken into high hills, with uncommonly deep valleys." The emigrants would not see the mighty Columbia again until they reached the Dalles.

Unfortunately, though the road improved, relations with the natives did not. The Indians along this river had experienced several years of exposure to the white man and his ways and that contact had bred little more than contempt. Unlike the natives the emigrants had met along the Snake River or in the Rockies, these people no longer held a fair skin individual in awe or even felt him worthy of respect. Instead, it was the Indian who used and abused the white man instead of the other way around.

Tallmadge Wood wrote his friends back in New York, "The Indians on the Columbia are a cowardly, thievish, indolent race of beings." Daniel Waldo declared, "We had no trouble with Indians until we got here among the missionaries then they began to steal." Jim Nesmith recorded that a Hudson's Bay man warned him to be on guard since he and his traveling companions were such a small group and the Indians "were very saucy, having three days ago robbed five men of all they had, at the same time drawing their bows and arrows and threatening to use them if the men did not give up their property."

John Shively, in following the overland route to the Dalles, claimed, "robberies were an everyday occurrence until we reached the Dall[e]s. If the party robbed made no resistance, the Indians would let him retain what he had on his back, and also his pony, nor did they whip any that made no resistance." S.M. Gilmore in a letter back to the states intended to encourage emigration admitted, "some of the emigrants were imposed on, in fact, some of them were robbed, though it was their own fault for not sticking together."

But even those who did stay together only found the Indians

using a different approach. Since the natives loved the white man's clothes they would steal a horse and then, when the emigrant reported it missing, innocently promise to find it in exchange for a shirt. The emigrants soon caught on to this game, however, and while at Waiilatpu, one of them, T.D. Kaiser, became so exasperated:

> . . . *[he] called a council of the chiefs and told them that he had paid his last shirt to have his horses brought back after being stolen by the Indians and that he would shoot every Indian he saw around camp after dark, after which there were no more horses stolen from his company.*

A more subtle form of robbery practiced by the Columbia River Indians consisted of insisting that the emigrants employ and compensate all natives in the vicinity before any one of them would work for pay. Since the Indians normally traveled in large bands, this made it nearly impossible to hire only a few hands in cases of need.

The emigrants were not the only ones who found the natives surly. John Charles Frémont was traveling in parallel with the land-based wagon-train as it moved towards the Dalles, and he reported:

> . . . *[the natives] manifested a not very friendly disposition, in several attempts to steal our horses. . . . I expected to find a badly disposed band, who had plundered a party of 14 emigrant men a few days before, and taken away their horses . . . but happily met with no difficulty.*

He frequently met with bands of them on the road since, "they were collected at every favorable spot along the river." Like the emigrants he found much to dislike:

> *In comparison with the Indians of the Rocky Mountains and*

the great eastern plain these are disagreeably dirty in their habits. Their huts were crowded with half-naked women and children, and the atmosphere within anything but pleasant to persons who had just been riding in the fresh morning air.

The overland passage from Fort Walla Walla required crossing three rivers and several minor streams. The rivers in succession were the Umatilla, the John Day, and the Deschutes. It was late enough in the year that each of these streams was fordable, although Frémont described the Deschutes as difficult. Looming ahead, however, was the Cascade Range. The emigrants could now see for themselves that what they had heard earlier was correct. Crossing those peaks, especially this late in the year, would be impossible.

John Arthur wrote; "owing to the lateness of the season, it was thought to be unwise for the emigrating party to undertake to make a wagon road over the Cascade Mountains, lest the way might be blockaded with snow and women and children perish with cold and hunger." They would have to travel by water from here.

It would be easy to sympathize with the emigrants at this point in their labors. They had worked so hard to get to the promised land and now that it lay less than 100 miles away, many must have thought it hardly worth the effort. They were bone weary, disenchanted with the land, pestered at every turn by the natives, and disappointed in their dealings with resident whites. How much more could they take? They did not know, of course, that for some of them the worst was yet to come.

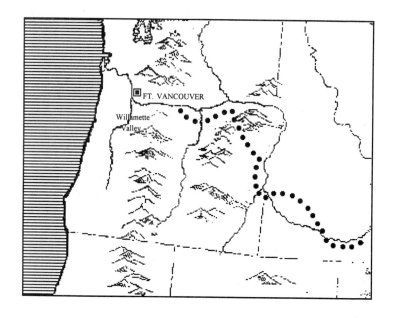

The Final Days

I

A strict chronology is meaningless in the final leg of the journey to the Willamette Valley in 1843. The emigrants had scattered to such an extent near the end that some of them finished their journey as early as October 27 (Jim Nesmith), while others struggled on until the end of November (Edward Lenox). Much of the time was taken up in building rafts, either at Fort Walla Walla or at the Dalles, moving stock overland to Oregon City, or simply resting at mission sites. The Burnetts and Applegates, for instance, spent three weeks in the vicinity of Waiilatpu and Fort Walla Walla, disposing of their animals and wagons and securing or building boats.

They were among those who decided to save themselves 120 miles of overland travel and embark at the mouth of the Walla Walla. Since many of them owned cattle, the Hudson's Bay man in charge, McKinsey, offered a special service. He agreed to exchange livestock head for head and sex for sex, in sharp contrast to the deal offered at the Whitman mission. Any emigrant wishing to take advantage of the opportunity was given a voucher representing a claim on livestock at the Hudson's Bay post at Fort Vancouver.

The one problem with the deal was that the cattle received in trade were a Spanish breed and far inferior to the emigrant's animals. When Applegate, for instance, presented his claim to Dr. McLoughlin at Fort Vancouver, that good man realized the disservice McKinsey was offering and refused to allow it. Instead, he permitted Applegate to retrieve his own herd from Walla Walla the following spring without charge for pasturage or care.

Daniel Waldo claimed there were no American cattle in Oregon until the emigration of 1843 arrived. As a result, the same cows that brought $48 a head in Missouri were worth $100 in Oregon. By contrast, Spanish cattle sold for $9. This episode not only reveals the generosity of McLoughlin, but shows as well how once again the personnel of the Hudson's Bay Company went out of their way to support the emigration, though it was not in their best interest to do so.

As it turned out, the cattle dealings at Walla Walla and Waiilatpu were the least of the problems that those emigrants who chose the water route had to face. Their real concern soon became the river itself. The placid-looking Columbia tempted many weary travelers into an experience they wished they had never begun.

Overton Johnson, for instance, disposed of his animals at Fort Walla Walla and with his companions purchased several Indian canoes as well as the services of a guide. As he explained:

The River, up and down from the Fort, as far as we could see, was broad and smooth, and we promised ourselves an agreeable passage, but we soon found that it was full of rocks, whirlpools, and dangerous rapids, to follow through which in safety required the greatest exertion, watchfulness and care. Our minds were constantly filled with anxiety and dread, and the wild manner in which our savage guide warned us of approaching danger had no tendency to dispel our unpleasant feelings.

As mentioned, Peter Burnett, too, chose to move his family and belongings down the river. He purchased an old boat that the Hudson's Bay Company had built expressly to navigate the Columbia. It was large enough to carry a considerable load yet light enough that natives could carry it easily around any stretch of the river requiring a portage. Burnett described it as about forty-five feet long, five feet wide, and three feet deep. For the journey down-stream, he employed an Indian pilot who stood in the bow of the boat with a long, broad paddle. In the stern Burnett's old friend William Beagle held a long steering oar, such as he had used in guiding flat-bottom boats back home.

Burnett related that Beagle had confidence in his ability to steer the boat based on his experience in passing through the rapids of the Ohio River. He continued, "But those rapids were nothing to those on the Columbia. I have seen Beagle turn pale as a corpse when passing through the terrible rapids on this river." They quickly learned to rely completely upon their Indian pilot, whom Burnett described as "cool, determined, and intrepid."

The Applegates, meanwhile, built their own boats for the trip to Fort Vancouver after whipsawing driftwood logs into lumber for material. They also hired a pilot to guide them but only the lead boat had such an experienced hand.

Lindsay Applegate's son, Jesse, then seven years old, later

described the initial days on the river as idyllic. Especially in contrast to, "traveling all summer bare foot through the desert sands, through sage brush, grease wood, and cactus." All went well, despite the fearsome rapids, until the families neared the Dalles. Jesse relates what happened then:

At the head of [the] rapids the river bears from a west course a little northerly, making a very gradual curve. As we approached this bend I could hear the sound of the rapids, and presently the boat began to rise and fall and rock from side to side. When we began to make the turn I could see breakers ahead extending in broken lines across the river, and the boat began to sweep along at a rapid rate. The pilot squatted low in the bow. An old red handkerchief was tied around his head and his long black hair hung down his back. There were now breakers on the right and on the left, and occasionally foam-crested waves swept across our bows. . . . I began to think this was no ordinary rapid, but felt reassured when I noticed that the older people sat quietly in their places and betrayed no sign of fear. . . . Our boat now was about twenty yards from the right-hand shore; when looking across the river I saw a smaller boat about opposite to us near the south bank. The persons in this boat were Alexander McClellan, about seventy years old, William Parker, probably twenty-one, and William Doke, about the same age, and three boys: Elisha Applegate, aged about eleven, and Warren and Edward Applegate, each about nine years old. This boat now near the south shore . . . should have followed our boat as the pilot was with us, and this was the dangerous part of the river. But there was little time to consider mistakes or to be troubled about what might be the consequences, for presently there was a wail of anguish, a shriek, and a scene of confusion in our boat that no language can describe. The boat we were watching disappeared and we saw the men and boys struggling in the water.

In this tragic accident three persons drowned: Alexander McClellan and the two younger Applegate boys, the sons of Jesse and Lindsay. Their bodies were never recovered. Lindsay Applegate, writing of the incident thirty-one years later, remembered, "At the time of the disaster it was utterly impossible to render them any assistance for it was only with the greatest skill that we succeeded in saving the women and children from sharing the same fate. It was a painful scene beyond description."

For the Applegates, of course, this was a tragedy of monumental proportions. They could never forget it; so, in 1846 they set out to pioneer a new route into Oregon that would by-pass that dreadful river. Though their trail, too, had its problems initially, it eventually became an effective alternate route into southern Oregon known as the Applegate Trail.

Peter Burnett, also experienced a tragic loss in his extended family while on the Columbia passage. Sara Jane Hill relates:

Peter H. Burnett sent his negro girl to the river after a bucket of water the river was running high as the wind was blowing hard, it was supposed she threw her bucket as a wave came up and when it succeeded it took her in as she never was seen again.

Only a stroke of luck prevented an additional drowning episode; Overton Johnson wrote:

On the first day after leaving the Fort, one of our canoes, in which there were three persons, one of whom was a lady, in passing through a narrow shoot in the Grand Rapids, struck a rock, upset and filled instantly. The lady and her husband succeeded in gaining the rock, which was about three feet across the top, and just under the surface of the water. Our pilot succeeded in taking them off in safety, and regained most of the property.

162

The Dalles Mission

The unfortunate participants in this drama were none other than William Newby and his wife. Fortunately for history, Newby's priceless diary was part of the property saved.

In one short passage the emigration lost four lives and barely avoided losing more. And they still had sixty or more miles of the Columbia to cover, including a portage around the falls of the Cascades.

II

The two arms of the emigration merged for one last time at the Methodist mission at the Dalles to begin the final leg of their journey downstream to Fort Vancouver.

The mission owed its existence to Jason Lee, the first missionary to arrive in the territory. Lee had begun his work in the Willamette Valley in 1834 but after receiving reinforcements in 1838 had expanded his operations to include the Dalles. It was an ideal location for his work since the course of the river provided here a natural fishing site that attracted Indians in large numbers.

Frémont provided a convenient description of the Dalles of the Columbia in his official report:

The whole volume of the river at this place passed between the walls of a chasm, which has the appearance of having been rent through the basaltic strata which form the valley rock of the region. At the narrowest place we found the breadth, by measurement, fifty-eight yards, and the average height of the walls above the water twenty-five feet; forming a trough between the rocks — whence the name, probably applied by a Canadian voyageur.

As far as wagon travel is concerned, the Oregon Trail ended at the Dalles in 1843. The emigrants who had trailed this far overland had reached the end of the road for their wheels. It would be three more years before a wagon road would be available to reach the Willamette Valley.

At the Dalles, those emigrants who still had wagons sent their cattle on ahead with drovers while they broke down their vehicles and placed them on rafts for transport the remaining distance. Ninevah Ford described the process:

Several of us went into the pine forest there and got dry pine trees and hauled them to the river with our oxen and made rafts of logs; six or eight, one foot to 18 inches diameter, and 20 feet long lashed together. We took our wagons apart and put the bodies on first and put the running gear on the top pieces and the baggage and stuff on top of that and lashed it on. Some would reserve a wagon bed with a cover on for a kind of a cabin for the women and children to sleep in.

From the Dalles, the emigrants drifted on their rafts some 50 miles over a pleasing stretch of placid water until they reached the treacherous falls of the Columbia, called the Cascades. Here they would face their final trial in a long Trail filled with trials. N. Bogart had dramatic memories of that last passage:

When they embarked the women felt as if they were facing

death as never before, they took their places . . . looking as stolid and indifferent as their dusky oarsmen, all their enthusiasm and finer feelings crushed out by the hardships all ready experienced. When trying to pass some of the Cascades, their frail craft would get caught in one of the many whirlpools, the water dashing over them, and drenching them through and through. Then the men would plunge in the cold stream and carry the half drowned women and children ashore, build huge bon-fires so they could partially dry themselves and goods, then proceed again on foot, the mothers clambering over rocks and fallen timber carrying the smallest child in their arms, with one or two clinging to their skirts, whilst the men would help tow the boats to smoother water.

They soon found the Cascades totally impassable for their cumbersome boats and rafts. As Overton Johnson explained:

Here the River, compressed into two thirds of its usual width, descends over huge rocks several hundred yards, with an inclination of about five degrees; and from the head to the foot of the Rapids, a distance of about four miles, the water descends about fifty feet. From the great agitation of the water, caused by its rushing with such velocity down its rocky channel, the surface of the River, for several hundred yards, is as white as a field of snow. On the South the dark basaltic walls, rising perpendicularly four or five hundred feet, are covered with Pines. There are small islands of rock, both above and below the Falls, many of which are timbered, and huge volcanic fragments cover either shore.

Peter Burnett remarked that he learned from the Indians in the area that according to their oral histories the Cascades had not existed a hundred years before and the river had been a series of rapids from the Dalles to that point. He continued:

This tradition said that the river gradually cut under the

165

mountain until the projecting mass of huge stones and tough clay slid into the river and dammed up the stream to the height of some thirty feet, thus producing the slack water to the Dalles. And I must say that every appearance, to my mind, sustains this view.

Portage was the only way around, and though it was but a short distance, because of the terrain the effort was considerable. Ninevah Ford, who had brought his wagons on the raft with him, said that at the Cascades he and others abandoned their rafts and spent two weeks building a road around the rapids so they could move their wagons. Then, on the other side of the Cascades:

I made a raft of 4 canoes lashing them side by side, taking the waggon beds of 5 waggon to pieces making a platform on top of the canoes, and then taking the running gears apart and putting them on top of the platform, and the baggage on top of the running gears. I lashed it all on securely and hoisted a mast in the center of the craft with a waggon sheet for a sail.

With two Indians and two white-men besides myself we set sail for the Vancouver. Those were the first waggons brought down the river below the Cascades.

Those without the resourcefulness of Ninevah Ford faced a difficult prospect. Many were destitute and without provisions. But they were not without friends. The Hudson's Bay headquarters, Fort Vancouver, stood 40 miles below the falls on the north bank of the Columbia and it was in command of a man who became a saint to the 1843 emigration, Dr. John McLoughlin.

That marvelous man learned from early arrivals of the plight of many people at the foot of the falls; so, he dispatched two boats loaded with provisions to provide assistance. Years later, William Newby told a reporter:

Arriving at the Cascades, [the emigrants] found that the generous Dr. McLoughlin had sent up batteaux to take the party to Fort Vancouver. There they found Mr. Douglass, the second in command, who gave the party a hearty reception. The Indian squaw wives were hustled out of some of the houses, and they were cleaned up and prepared for the families. Food and fuel, and every needed supply were furnished. Here they were gladdened by the sight of ripe, fresh apples which they had not seen since they left their far-distant home. As soon as rested they were taken in batteaux to Oregon City, where they were landed on the 6th of November, 1843, and not a cent was charged for all that trouble and splendid treatment at Fort Vancouver. . . . And this was not all. Some of the party were very sick and worn out by the hardships of the long journey, and remained in the hospital at Fort Vancouver, receiving medical attention, nursing and every attention, and no charge made for anything.

Fort Vancouver was unlike the earlier forts along the trail. Here the emigrants could find plentiful supplies and services such as they might have expected in the states. (Narcissa Whitman, in 1836, called the fort the New York of the Pacific Ocean.) Most importantly, however, they could lean upon the strength of the Hudson's Bay Company. This powerful company had had the Oregon territory all to themselves for many years. In that time, they had subdued the land and the natives, established a system of laws and justice, and laid the groundwork for a new civilization. To their regret, however, they had been unsuccessful in enticing emigration from England or Canada to take advantage of their primary position. That failing and the tenacity of the American emigrants sealed the fate of Oregon eventually to become part of the United States.

The emigrants truly were back in civilization. This aspect of the Oregon trail experience is another way in which it differed from the pioneering efforts of earlier generations. Instead of leaving civilization and plunging into a wild unsettled frontier, the Oregon emigrants crossed an untamed wilderness only to return to civilized life. That distinction by no means diminishes their accomplishment, however; it remains one of the most extraordinary events in recorded history.

The great experiment had been far more difficult than anyone had expected. They had left Elm Grove in the spring in sunshine and song and arrived at Fort Vancouver in the late fall in darkness and lament, but the passage of time would reveal that in the process they had turned the tide of history. No one gave that any thought in November of 1843, of course. They were far too weary and apprehensive to engage in such idle fancy. And many were too sad. But some day they would all have reason to be proud of what they had done. After all, there would be another spring and there was a new life to begin.

When the Great Migration left Missouri for Oregon in the spring of 1843, many members of the wagon train had joined the adventure because of the free land bill then pending in congress. It would take more than a year for those people to learn that the bill never got out of the House of Representatives.

Upon their arrival in the Willamette Valley, the emigrants did learn, however, that a handful of old Oregon settlers had formed a provisional government while they were on the trail. While the history behind that act is beyond the scope of this story, suffice it to say that the settlers acted out of desperation. They had grown tired of waiting for the United States and Great Britain to arrive at an agreement with respect to the Oregon country; and they needed some form of government.

The new legislative body did believe that the United States eventually would declare sovereignty over them so they, like many of the emigrants, assumed that the land grants spoken of in Senator Linn's bill eventually would become law. Acting in good faith, then, they authorized land claims accordingly. It took several years to resolve the resulting confusion.

When Oregon did become an official territory of the United States in 1848, the first task their territorial representatives assumed was to lobby strenuously to have Congress recognize the existing land claims. It was not until 1850, however, that they achieved any success. In that year Congress finally passed a special bill for the Oregon Territory called the Donation Land Law. Even then, the bill authorized only 320 acres for each claimant instead of the 640 the provisional government had allowed. Married men, though, could claim an additional 320 acres for their wife.

The Donation Land Law was the first free land bill in the history of the United States, preceding the Homestead Act by a dozen years. It was scheduled originally to expire at the end of 1853 but as that date neared, Congress passed an extension to last through 1855. A peculiar sidelight to Oregon history was the extraordinary number of marriages that occurred in 1855 just before the land act became history.

Land claims were not the only problems the new emigrants had to face. The economy did not prove as healthy as they had hoped. The Hudson's Bay Company was a dependable source of business at first, but as emigration continued that business became spread too thin. Further, in 1846, when the United States and Great Britain finally resolved the boundary dispute at the 49th parallel, the HBC moved their headquarters to Vancouver Island thus diminishing business even more.

The situation looked increasingly dire until the discovery of gold in California. That proved to be a salvation, not only because the Oregonians were close by and could move quickly to take advantage of the opportunities in the gold fields, but also because those who stayed at home now had a new, insatiable market for their agricultural products.

Among those who left for California during the gold rush was Peter Burnett. He became that state's first governor when it was admitted to the union in 1850. Diarist Pierson Reading also prospered in the golden state; the town of Redding, California is named for him. Jim Nesmith and William Newby stayed in Oregon, Jim becoming one of the first to represent his state in the United States Senate while Newby served in the State Senate and founded the town of McMinnville. John Shively also remained in Oregon to lay out the town of Astoria where, in 1847, he became the first postmaster west of the Rocky Mountains. One other noted participant in the events of 1843, though not an emigrant himself, John Charles Frémont, became first a Senator from California and, in 1856, the first candidate for president from the newly formed Republican party.

Diligent research would undoubtedly reveal other such success stories, yet one of the most intriguing questions about the Great Migration would remain unanswered; that is, what kind of people made the trip? We have had an opportunity to become acquainted with a few individuals through their diaries and reminiscences but they represent only a minuscule portion of the nearly 1000 people involved. The question becomes more important when we examine

170

contemporary evidence for a wider view. It is not flattering.

For instance, the Hudson's Bay Company before moving their headquarters in 1846, installed cannons in the bastions of Fort Vancouver out of alarm over the type of people they saw arriving in the yearly emigrations. Narcissa Whitman, in 1846, wrote of the emigrants she had seen, "There are many intelligent and excellent people, and also many who are lawless and ignorant." That same year, Francis Parkman, author of one of the most famous works on the Oregon trail, had occasion to visit with a group of emigrants at Fort Laramie and found, "for the most part, they were the rudest and most ignorant of the frontier population."

Rude, ignorant, lawless? How does that square with the roles of governor, senator, postmaster, town-founder? Probably Narcissa was right when she said there were both kinds. We will never know, but one historian who had occasion to meet with and interview many of the participants in the Great Migration in their later years had this to say:

The immigration of 1843 was composed of people of pronounced character, rudely arrogant and aggressive rather than tame and submissive.

People of pronounced character! If only she had stopped there. Surely, even the emigrants themselves would have been pleased with that.

Chapter One: Catching the Fever

1. According to one study: Bell, *Opening a Highway to the Pacific*,119 (hereafter cited as Bell)

1. "twelve months ago": Baker, Abner S. III, *Experience, Personality and Memory,* Oregon Historical Quarterly, Vol. LXXXI, 236 (hereafter Baker-OHQ)

1. Wheat was selling: Bell, 124-125

1. And Jesse had recently sold: Waldo, *Critiques*, 10 (hereafter Waldo)

2. Nesmith quote: *Transactions of the Oregon Pioneer Association* (OPAT), 1876, 52 (hereafter OPAT)

3. "Take what may be necessary": Burnett, *Recollections and Opinions of an Old Pioneer,* OHQ, Vol. V, 65 (hereafter Recollections)

3. Applegate long quote: Applegate, *Views of Oregon History,* 22 (hereafter Views)

3. "No tie of near kindred': OPAT, 52

4. "set to work most vigorously": Recollections, 65

4. Lenox long quote: Lenox, *Overland to Oregon,* 13 (hereafter Lenox)

5. Gregg long quote: Gregg, *Commerce of the Prairies,* 23 (hereafter Gregg)

6. "too much like all small villages": Talbot, *The Journal of Theodore Talbot,* 6 (hereafter Talbot)

6. "a constant source of interest": Field, *Prairie & Mountain Sketches,* 25 (hereafter Field)

6. Field long quote: ibid

7. Nesmith quote: OPAT, 45

7. "The Oregon fever is raging": Documents, OHQ, Vol IV, 175

8. "The migration of a large body": Applegate, *A Day with the Cow Column in 1843,* OHQ, Vol I, 371 (hereafter Cow Column)

8. Greeley long quote: cited in Unruh, *The Plains Across,*10

8. "species of madness": Baker-OHQ, 237

12. Benton quote: Benton, *Thirty Years View,* 470

12. McDuffie quote: ibid, 471
13. Linn speech: ibid, 472
13. Burnett quote: Recollections., 64
13. Ford quote: Ford, *The Pioneer Road Makers,* 2 (hereafter Ford)
13. "this is the proper way": Niles Register, Vol 64, 121
14. "Whoo Ha!": Bright, *The Folklore and History of the "Oregon Fever,"* OHQ, Vol LII, 241

Chapter Two: Preparing to Go

15. "the patience of Job": Berry, *A Majority of Scoundrels,* 236 (hereafter Berry)
16. Boardman quote: Boardman, *The Journal of John Boardman,* Utah Historical Quarterly, Vol 2, Number 4, 99 (hereafter UHQ)
17. Looney quote: Looney, *Told by the Pioneers,* Vol 1, 75 (hereafter Looney)
17. Burnett quote: Burnett, *Letters of Peter H. Burnett,* OHQ, Vol III, 418 (hereafter Letters)
18. Gilmore quotes: Documents, OHQ, Vol IV, 282 (hereafter OHQ)
19. Gregg quote: Gregg, 25
20. Boardman quotes: UHQ, 100, 102, 103, 113
21. Burnett long quote: Letters, 418
21. Gilmore quotes: OHQ, 282
21. Looney quote: Looney, 75
22. Burnett quote: Letters, 419
23. Gilmore quotes: OHQ, 282
23. Looney quotes: Looney, 75
24. Gilmore quote: OHQ, 282
25. formal agreement: Letters, 406-407

Chapter Three: The Epic Journey Begins

27. Applegate quote: Cow Column, 373
28. Nesmith quote: Nesmith, *Diary of the Emigration of 1843,* OHQ, Vol VII, 330 (hereafter Diary)
28. Reading quote: Reading, *Journal of Pierson Barton Reading,* Journal of the Society of California Pioneers, 1930, 149 (hereafter JSCP)

28. One historian who studied: Faragher, *Women and Men on the Overland Trail,* 163

29. Another historian agreed: Schlissel, *Women's Diaries of the Westward Journey, 155*

29. Burnett quote: Recollections, 65

29. Waldo quote: Waldo, 11

29. "Tales of rich lands": Newby, *William T. Newby's Diary of the Emigration of 1843,* OHQ, Vol XL, 219 (hereafter Newby)

29. Looney quote: Looney, 76

30. Burnett on Elm Grove: Letters, 405

30. Burnett long quote: Recollections, 67

31. Reading quote: JSCP, 150

31. "this produced great": Letters, 409

31. "in a new and trying": Recollections, 66

32. Sara Hill long quote: Hill, manuscript in Oregon Historical Society Library, 1 (hereafter Hill)

32. Reading quote: JSCP, 150

33. Kaiser quote: Kaiser, *How we Made the Emigrant Road,* Bancroft Library, 1

33. Drowning incident: Diary, 330, Lenox, 22

33. Lenox quote: Lenox, 22

Chapter Four: A Moving Community

34. Reading: JSCP, 150

35. McCarver quote: Documents, OHQ, Vol II, 191

35. Gilpin quote: ibid, 192

35. Reading quote: JSCP, 150

35. Newby quote: Newby, 222

36. long quote: Field, 26-27

37. "glib-tongued orator": OPAT, 46

37. Reading quote: JSCP, 151

37. McCarver quote: Documents, OHQ, Vol IV, 177

38. A few years ago, a prominent historian: Stewart, Geo. R., *Prairie Schooner Got Them There,* American Heritage, Vol 13, 101

38. Shively long quote: List, Howard M. & Edith M. eds., *John M. Shively's Memoir, Part I,* OHQ, Vol LXXXI, 16 (hereafter Shively)

40. Burnett quotes: Recollections, 66

Chapter Five: Stormy Weather

41. Johnson quote: Johnson, Overton and Winter, Wm. H., *Route Across the Rocky Mountains,* OHQ, Vol VII, 69 (hereafter J&W)
42. Newby quote: Newby, 222
42. Reading quotes: JSCP, 155
42. Hill quotes: Hill, 2-3
43. Boardman quotes: UHQ, 100
43. Owens quotes: Owens-Adair, Dr., *Mrs. Sarah Damron Adair, Pioneer of 1843,* OPAT, 1900, 69 (hereafter Owens)
43. Burnett quote: Recollections, 66
43. Lenox quote: Lenox, 25
43. Stoughton quote: Oliphant, J. Orin, *Passing of an Immigrant of 1843,* Washington Historical Quarterly, July 1924, 206 (hereafter Stoughton)
43. Burnett resignation: Letters, 410, Recollections 68
44. Applegate long quote #1: Views, 8
44. Applegate long quote #2: Cow Column, 373
45. Applegate long quote: ibid, 372-374
47. Burnett quote: Letters, 410
47. Hill quote: Hill, 4
47. Lenox long quote: Lenox, 37-38
54. Burnett quote: Letters, 412
54. Nesmith quote: Diary, 332
54. Reading quote: JSCP, 157
55. Jesse Applegate long quote: Applegate, Jesse A., *Recollections of My Boyhood,* 114 (hereafter Jesse)
55. Johnson quote #1: J&W, 70
55. Johnson quote #2: ibid, 74
55. Reading quote: JSCP, 158
56. Burnett quote: Letters, 412

Chapter Seven: The Platte River Road

57. "beautiful prairie country": JSCP, 158
58. Burnett quote: Letters, 413
58. Reading quote: JSCP, 158
58. Burnett long quote: Recollections, 71

59. Applegate long quote: Cow Column, 379
60. Jesse Applegate long quote: Jesse, 112-113
60. Burnett quote: Letters, 414
61. Hill long quote: Hill, 10
62. Burnett quote: Recollections, 72
62. Johnson long quote: J & W, 72-73
62. Nesmith quote: Diary, 334
63. Reading quotes: JSCP, 159

Chapter Eight: The South Platte Crossing

66. Reading quote: JSCP, 160
66. Newby quote: Newby, 224
66. Boardman quote: UHQ, 101
66. Johnson long quote: J & W, 75
66. Nesmith long quote: Diary, 336
67. Reading quote: JSCP, 161-162
67. Newby long quote: Newby, 224
68. Owens long quote: Owens, 69-70
68. Stoughton long quote: Stoughton, 206
68. Penter long quote: Penter, Samuel, *Recollections of an Oregon Pioneer of 1843,* OHQ, Vol VII, 59
69. "without any serious accident": J & W, 75

Chapter Nine: The Missionary Doctor

71. Reading quote: JSCP, 162
71. Nesmith quote: Diary, 337
72. Nesmith long quote #1: ibid
72. Reading quote: JSCP, 163
72. Nesmith long quote #2: Diary, 338
73. Reading long quote: JSCP, 161
73. Waldo quote: Waldo, 16-17
76. Applegate quote: Cow Column, 381
76. Nesmith quote: cited in Drury, Clifford M., *Marcus Whitman, M.D.,* 334
76. Arthur quote: Arthur, John, *A Brief Account of the Experiences of a Pioneer of 1843,* OPAT, 1887, 97 (hereafter Arthur)
76. correspondent long quote: Documents, OHQ, Vol IV, 170

Chapter Ten: Sights Along the North Platte

78. Nesmith quote: Diary, 338
78. Reading: JSCP, 163
79. "Travel, travel, travel;": Cow Column, 381
80. Johnson long quote: J & W, 76
80. Reading long quote: JSCP, 164
81. Nesmith quote: Diary, 339
81. Newby quote: Newby, 225
81. Reading quote: JSCP, 165
81. Johnson quote: J & W, 76
82. reporter's story: Fields, 64-65

Chapter Eleven: Fort Laramie

84. Nesmith quote: Diary, 340
85. Burnett long quote: 74-75
86. Frémont quote: Nevins, Allan ed., *Narratives of Exploration and Adventure,* by John Charles Frémont, 131 (hereafter Nevins)
86. Narcissa Whitman quote: Elliott, T.C. , *The Coming of the White Women,* OHQ, Vol XXXVII, 283
87. Nesmith quote: Diary, 340
88. Burnett quote: Recollections, 74
88. Reading quote: JSCP, 165
88. Nesmith long quote: OPAT, 53
89. "After traveling for some time": OPAT, 1897, 98
89. Looney quote: Looney, 76
89. Newby quote: Newby, 226
89. Johnson quote: J & W, 78
90. Newby quotes: Newby, 227
90. Nesmith long quote: Diary, 342

Chapter Twelve: Independence Rock

92. Johnson quote: J & W, 78-79
93. Johnson quotes: ibid, 79
94. Johnson long quote: ibid
95. Nesmith long quote: Diary, 344

95. Nesmith quote: ibid

Chapter Thirteen: Death, Disease, and Acts of Deity

96. Nesmith quotes: Diary, 344
97. Boardman quote: UHQ, 104
97. Nesmith long quote: Diary, 344
97. Reading quote: JSCP, 170
98. Hill quote: Hill, 6
99. Nesmith quote: Diary, 345
99. "We buried him": Recollections, 75
99. "a grand and magnificent sight": ibid
99. Newby quote: Newby, 229
99. Johnson long quote: J & W, 83
100. Talbot long quote: Talbot, 38
100. Nesmith quote: Diary, 345
101. "a loud, sharp report": Diary, 346
101. "one clap of thunder": UHQ, 106
101. Newby long quote: Newby, 228-229

Chapter Fourteen: South Pass

102. Johnson quote: J & W, 86
103. "on the very height": UHQ, 108
103. Newby quote: Newby, 229
105. Nesmith quote: Diary, 347
105. Talbot quote: Talbot, 40
106. Reading quote: JSCP, 171-172

Chapter Fifteen: Fort Bridger

107. Hill long quote: Hill, 8
108. Shively long quote: Shively, 17-18
109. Burnett quote: Letters, 417
110. Bridger long quote: Paden, Irene D., *The Wake of the Prairie Schooner, 246-247* (hereafter Paden)
110. Johnson quote: J & W, 86
110. Boardman quote: UHQ, 107
111. Nesmith long quote: Diary, 348

111. Newby quote: Newby, 231
111. Burnett: Recollections, 76

Chapter Sixteen: The Bear River Valley

112. Reading quote: JSCP, 173
112. "good and fat": UHQ, 107
113. Johnson quotes: J & W, 87
113. Frémont long quote: Nevins, 217-218
114. Reading quote: JSCP, 174
114. Talbot long quote: 45
114. Nesmith long quote: Diary, 349
115. Reading quote: JSCP, 174
115. Newby quote: Newby, 231
115. Frémont quote: Nevins, 221
115. Talbot long quote: 46
115. Newby quote: Newby, 231

Chapter Seventeen: Fort Hall

116. Talbot quote: 47
117. Wyeth statement: Berry, 400
119. Reading quote: JSCP, 175
120. Burnett quotes: Recollections, 77

Chapter Eighteen: The First Wagons West

123. letter to Sec. Eaton: *Report of Smith, Jackson, and Sublette (1830) etc.,* 21st Congress, 2nd session, Senate Doc. No. 39
124. "it was a greater wonder": Whitman, Narcissa Prentiss, *My Journal,* 16 (hereafter Narcissa)
124. "They are so resolute": ibid, 18
125. "Perhaps you will wonder": ibid, 32
126. Newell re Harris: Haines, Francis, *Pioneer Portraits: Robert Newell,* Idaho Yesterdays, Spring, 1965, 5 (hereafter Haines)
126. Whitman quote: Elliot, T.C., *"Doctor" Robert Newell: Pioneer,* OHQ, Vol IX, 107
126. Newell long quote: Haines, 6

Chapter Nineteen: The Snake River Plateau

128. Burnett: Recollections, 78
129. Talbot long quote: Talbot, 53
129. Newby: Newby, 233
129. Boardman quote: UHQ, 113
129. Boardman long quote: 112-113
130. Frémont long quote: Nevins, 261, 265
130. Shively statement: Shively, 18-19
131. Johnson quotes: J & W, 91-92
131. Talbot quote: Talbot, 54
131. Frémont long quote: Nevins, 270
131. Johnson long quote: J & W, 92
132. Newby statement: Newby, 233
132. Owens quotes: 70-71
133. Lenox statements: Lenox, 50
133. Stoughton long quote: Stoughton, 207-208
134. Johnson quote: J & W, 92-93
134. Boardman quote: UHQ, 113
134. Newby quotes: Newby, 234

Chapter Twenty: Fort Boise

136. Boardman quote: UHQ, 113
137. "a very agreeable": Diary, 352
137. "exceedingly polite": Talbot, 59
137. Fort description: Idaho Yesterdays, *Fort Boise,* Spring 1962, 35
137. Nesmith quote: Diary, 352
137. Newby statement: Newby, 235

Chapter Twenty-one: The Burnt River Canyon

139. Burnett: Recollections, 81
139. Frémont: Nevins, 280
139. Nesmith quote: Diary, 352
139. Burnett: Recollections, 81
139. Newby quote: Newby, 235
139. Hill statements: Hill, 11

140. Newby long quote: Newby, 235
140. Frémont quotes: Nevins, 281
140. Johnson long quote: J & W, 94
141. Burnett long quote #1: Recollections, 81
141. Crawford quote: Crawford, Medorem, *Journal of Medorem Crawford,* 18
141. Burnett long quote #2: Recollections, 81-82
142. Frémont long quote: Nevins, 282

Chapter Twenty-two: The Blue Mountain Crossing

143. Burnett quote: Recollections, 82
143. Ford quote: Ford, 10
144. Hill quote: Hill, 11
144. Burnett quote: Recollections, 82
144. Ford quote: Ford, 10
144. Newby quote: Newby, 236
144. Nesmith quote: Diary, 353
145. Ford long quote: Ford, 11
145. "wherever he directed": Ford, 12
145. Nesmith quotes: OPAT, 48
146. Burnett quote: Recollections, 82
146. Nesmith quote: Diary, 354-355

Chapter Twenty-three: The Whitman Mission

147. A historian once compared: Paden, 20
148. "one adobe house": Nevins, 289
149. Newby long quote: Newby, 237, 238
149. Waldo long quote: Waldo, 16
149. Hill quote: Hill, 13
149. Lenox, quote: Lenox, 54
150. McClane long quote: McClane mss in Bancroft Library, 6
150. Burnett long quote: Recollections, 82-83
151. Frémont long quote: Nevins, 290
152. Newby quote: Newby, 238
152. Nesmith quote: Diary, 355
153. Nesmith long quote: ibid
153. Frémont quotes: Nevins, 291-292

Chapter Twenty-four: The Columbia River Indians

155. Frémont quote: Nevins, 294
155. Wood quote: Documents, OHQ, Vol III, 397
155. Waldo quote: Waldo, 2
155. Nesmith quote: Diary, 356
155. Shively quote: Shively, 23
155. Gilmore quote: OHQ, 283
156. Kaiser quote: Kaiser, T.D., *Kaiser's Narrative*, 6-7
156. Frémont quotes: Nevins, 294, 292, 296
157. Arthur quote: Arthur, 98

Chapter Twenty-five: The Final Days

160. Johnson long quote: J & W, 97
160. Burnett quotes: Recollections, 83-84
161. Jesse Applegate quotes: Jesse, 143, 149-150
162. Lindsay Applegate quote: Applegate, L. *Notes and Reminiscences etc. in the Year 1846.* OHQ, Vol XXII, 13
162. Hill quote: Hill, 15
162. Johnson quote: J & W, 97
163. Frémont quote: Nevins, 296
164. Ford long quote: Ford, 14-15
164. Bogart long quote: Bogart, N. *Reminiscences of Pioneer Days.* manuscript, Washington State Historical Society, folder 24, 3-4
165. Johnson long quote: J & W, 100
165. Burnett long quote: Recollections, 88
166. Ford long quote: Ford, 17
167. Newby long quote: Newby, 240-241
167. Narcissa Whitman quote: Narcissa, 48

Epilogue

171. Narcissa Whitman quote: Whitman, Narcissa, *The Letters of Narcissa Whitman.* Ye Galleon Press, 211
171. Parkman quote: Parkman, Francis, *The Oregon Trail.* 102
171. "The immigration of 1843": Victor, F.F., Bancroft Historian, *History of Oregon, 1848-1888.*, 425

182

BIBLIOGRAPHY

Books Cited in Source Notes

Applegate, Jesse A. *Recollections of My Boyhood.* Roseburg: Press of Review Publishing Co., 1914

Applegate, Jesse *Views of Oregon History.* Yoncalla: 1878 (Oregon State University Library)

Bancroft, Hubert Howe, *The Works of Hubert Howe Bancroft.* San Francisco: The History Co. (*History of Oregon, 1848-1888.* Vol. XXX., 1888)

Bell, James Christy. *Opening a Highway to the Pacific 1838-1846.* New York: Columbia University, 1921

Berry, Don. *A Majority of Scoundrels.* Sausalito: A Comstock Edition, 1961

Benton, Thomas Hart. *Thirty Years View.* New York: 1854-1856

Carey, Charles H. ed., *The Journals of Theodore Talbot.* Portland: Metropolitan Press, 1931

Dodd, Lawrence L. ed., *My Journal 1836 by Narcissa Prentiss Whitman.* Fairfield: Ye Galleon Press, 1982

Drury, Clifford Merrill. *Marcus Whitman, M.D.* Caldwell, Idaho: Caxton Printers, 1937

Faragher, John Mack. *Women and Men on the Overland Trail.* New Haven: Yale University Press, 1979

Ford, Ninevah. *The Pioneer Road Makers.* Salem: 1878 (manuscript in Bancroft Library)

Gregg, Kate L. & McDermott, John Francis. ed., *Prairie and Mountain Sketches by Matthew C. Field.* Norman: University of Oklahoma Press, 1957

Kaiser, P. C. *How We Made the Emigrant Road.* Salem: 1878 (manuscript in Bancroft Library)

Moorhead, Max L. ed., *Commerce of the Prairies by Josiah Gregg.* Norman: University of Oklahoma Press, 1954

Nevins, Allan, ed., *Narratives of Exploration and Adventure by John Charles Frémont.* New York: Longmans, Green & Co., 1956

Paden, Irene D. *The Wake of the Prairie Schooner.* Carbondale: Southern Illinois University Press, 1943

Parkman, Francis. *The Oregon Trail.* New York: The Modern Library, 1949

Schlissel, Lillian. *Women's Diaries of the Westward Journey.* New York: Schocken Books, 1982

Told By the Pioneers. Vol. 1, 1937 (Washington State University Library)

Unruh, John D. *The Plains Across.* Chicago: University of Illinois Press, 1982

Waldo, Daniel. *Critiques.* Salem: 1878 (manuscript in Bancroft Library)

Whitaker, Robert. ed., *Overland to Oregon by Edward Henry Lenox.* Oakland: 1904

Whitman, Narcissa. *The Letters of Narcissa Whitman 1836-1847.* Fairfield: Ye Galleon Press, 1986

Young, F. G. ed., *Journal of Medorem Crawford.* Eugene: Star Job Office, 1897

ORDER FORM
"BLAZING A WAGON TRAIL TO OREGON"

Please send me_____copies of
Blazing a Wagon Trail to Oregon @
$12.95 per copy $_____

Shipping and Handling $ 1.00

Total $_____

Rush the order to:

Name:_____

Address:_____

City:_____ State:_____

Zip Code:_____

Send check or money order to:

Echo Books
P.O. Box 171
Enterprise, Oregon 97828
(503)962-5094